BARRON'S BOOK NOTES

DANTE ALIGHIERI'S

Divine Comedy: The Inferno

BY

Carol Forman

SERIES EDITOR

Michael Spring
Editor, *Literary Cavalcade*
Scholastic Inc.

BARRON'S EDUCATIONAL SERIES, INC.
Woodbury, New York / London / Toronto / Sydney

ACKNOWLEDGMENTS

We would like to acknowledge the many painstaking hours of work Holly Hughes and Thomas F. Hirsch have devoted to making the *Book Notes* series a success.

All inquiries should be addressed to:
Barron's Educational Series, Inc.
113 Crossways Park Drive
Woodbury, New York 11797

Library of Congress Catalog Card No. 84-18469

International Standard Book No. 0-8120-3411-2

Library of Congress Cataloging in Publication Data
Forman, Carol.
 Dante Alighieri's Divine comedy, The inferno.

 (Barron's book notes)
 Bibliography: p. 93
 Summary: A guide to reading "The Inferno" with a critical and appreciative mind encouraging analysis of plot, style, form, and structure. Also includes background on the author's life and times, sample tests, term paper suggestions, and a reading list.
  1. Dante Alighieri, 1265–1321. Inferno [1. Dante Alighieri, 1265–1321. Inferno. 2. Italian literature— History and criticism] I. Title.
P04443. F66 1984   851'.1   84-18469
ISBN 0-8120-3411-2 (pbk.)

PRINTED IN THE UNITED STATES OF AMERICA

456   550   987654321

CONTENTS

ADVISORY BOARD

HOW TO USE THIS BOOK

You have to know how to approach literature in order to get the most out of it. This *Barron's Book Notes* volume follows a plan based on methods used by some of the best students to read a work of literature.

Begin with the guide's section on the author's life and times. As you read, try to form a clear picture of the author's personality, circumstances, and motives for writing the work. This background usually will make it easier for you to hear the author's tone of voice, and follow where the author is heading.

Then go over the rest of the introductory material—such sections as those on the plot, characters, setting, themes, and style of the work. Underline, or write down in your notebook, particular things to watch for, such as contrasts between characters and repeated literary devices. At this point, you may want to develop a system of symbols to use in marking your text as you read. (Of course, you should only mark up a book you own, not one that belongs to another person or a school.) Perhaps you will want to use a different letter for each character's name, a different number for each major theme of the book, a different color for each important symbol or literary device. Be prepared to mark up the pages of your book as you read. Put your marks in the margins so you can find them again easily.

Now comes the moment you've been waiting for—the time to start reading the work of literature. You may want to put aside your *Barron's Book Notes* volume until you've read the work all the way through. Or you may want to alternate, reading the *Book Notes* analysis of each section as soon as you have finished reading the corresponding part of the original. Before you move on, reread crucial passages you don't fully understand. (Don't take this guide's analysis for granted—make up your own mind as to what the work means.)

Once you've finished the whole work of literature, you may want to review it right away, so you can firm up your ideas about what it means. You may want to leaf through the book concentrating on passages you marked in reference to one character or one theme. This is also a good time to reread the *Book Notes* introductory material, which pulls together insights on specific topics.

When it comes time to prepare for a test or to write a paper, you'll already have formed ideas about the work. You'll be able to go back through it, refreshing your memory as to the author's exact words and perspective, so that you can support your opinions with evidence drawn straight from the work. Patterns will emerge, and ideas will fall into place; your essay question or term paper will almost write itself. Give yourself a dry run with one of the sample tests in the guide. These tests present both multiple-choice and essay questions. An accompanying section gives answers to the multiple-choice questions as well as suggestions for writing the essays. If you have to select a term paper topic, you may choose one from the list of suggestions in this book. This guide also provides you with a reading list, to help you when you start research for a term paper, and a selection of provocative comments by critics, to spark your thinking before you write.

THE AUTHOR AND HIS TIMES

Have you ever spent long hours fantasizing some horrible punishment for a person who has done something bad to you? The torture must be perfect: painful, yet relating somehow to the specific wrong the person has done you.

Carry that fantasy to another level. Imagine everyone, past and present, good and bad, getting, finally, exactly what he or she deserves.

Back in the early 1300s in Italy, a man carried through with that fantasy—on paper, of course. He literally told everyone where to go, Hell, Purgatory, or Heaven, and went on to design specific punishments or rewards based on the life each person led. He laid them all end to end and then made himself a character (actually a not-too-bright lost soul) who walks the entire length of the universe.

The work is called the *Divine Comedy*. The author is Dante Alighieri.

Dante was born in Florence, Italy, in 1265. This would be one of those meaningless, soon forgotten facts if it were not so significant for the works Dante produced. It happened to be the wrong place at the wrong time.

At the time of Dante's birth, Florence was a prosperous city-state, full of greedy merchants, dedicated scholars, and warring political factions. The two most influential families in Florence were the Guelphs and the Ghibellines. The Guelphs were supporters of the Pope and the Ghibellines supported the German emperor, who claimed power in Italy. Shortly before

Dante was born, the Ghibellines were ousted from power, and the Guelphs, with whom Dante's family was associated, took power.

Dante began his own political career in 1295 when the Guelphs were firmly established and many of the Ghibellines were still in exile. At that time, however, a split began in the Guelphs; the two sides became known later as the Whites and the Blacks. The crisis came to a head in 1300 when the Whites, who were in power, decided to prosecute the Blacks who had gone to Rome to ask the Pope to intervene on their behalf. (Remember, the Guelphs had backed the Pope—he owed them a favor.) Dante was one of the six White leaders responsible for this decision. In 1301, the next year, the Blacks staged a successful coup and the White leaders, including Dante, were sent into exile. In 1302, charged with graft, hostility against the Pope, and a long list of other crimes, in his absence Dante was sentenced to death—if he was ever caught in Florence again.

Consequently, Dante never returned to his home city. This exile also meant that Dante's fortunes, which were not as large as his family had once held, were confiscated. He spent the remainder of his life living at the expense and generosity of friends. He died in Ravenna in 1321.

Dante's private life is less well defined than his public affairs. He was betrothed to Gemma Donati in 1277 (remember he would have been twelve then!) whom he later married. There were three children: Jacopo, Pietro, and Antonia. (Some of the historians mention a fourth, Giovanni.) When Dante's sons were fourteen, they also had to join their father in exile. Both Jacopo and Pietro later wrote about the *Divine Comedy*. Antonia entered a convent and took the name Sister Beatrice.

Dante wrote the *Divine Comedy* while he was in exile. He finished the first part, the *Inferno,* in 1314 and the final cantos of the *Paradiso* in 1320. The title of the entire work is *The Comedy of Dante Alighieri, Florentine by Citizenship, Not by Morals.*

Dante was a man who lived, who saw political and artistic success, and who was in love. He was also a man who was defeated, who felt the danger and humiliation of exile, and who was no stranger to the cruelty and treachery possible in people. Dante felt that he was the victim of a grave injustice. He also suffered serious self-doubts—natural for a man in exile and eternally dependent. Remembering all this about Dante, we can see his work as the sum of all these experiences and his answers to the basic human questions: What is man? Why does he act as he does? What is Good and what is Evil? When it so often looks like "Good guys finish last," why should anyone be good?

You are probably saying, "So what?" at this point. But trying to understand a work of literature is often a lot like trying to understand other people. You have to figure out where they are coming from and what makes them tick. Dante comes from a medieval Roman Catholic background, and that is extremely important for the *Divine Comedy.*

What if a reader is not a Catholic or a Christian? What about a 20th-century reader who doesn't know medieval history? Can that person still understand the poem, or will the religious and medieval aspects get in the way? Obviously, we can't promise there will never be a problem, but the work has been read all over the world for centuries.

After all, when you read science fiction, you accept that certain aliens may have certain amazing powers, or that a particular planet has different scientific laws than we have on earth. Science fiction authors use those unusual, supernatural possibilities as elements of their plots. So, too, Dante uses the concepts and symbols accepted in his age and his religion as elements around which to structure his story. You don't have to believe they are true in order to appreciate how they work in the poem. Let's examine some of the concepts Dante inherited from 14th-century Italy's way of thinking.

One feature of Dante's vision of the universe is the concept of polarities: two extreme opposites, between which people were pulled. To Dante, many aspects of his world were polar in nature:

1.   There was a power struggle between the Church and State, represented by the Pope and the German emperor.

2.   There was a struggle for intellectual authority between theology (the study of religion and the Bible) and philosophy (which included science and mathematics). Dante himself was a heavy borrower from both sides and quoted such diverse sources as the Greek philosophers Aristotle and Plato, or the Christian thinkers St. Augustine and St. Thomas Aquinas.

3.   Man was considered to fall halfway between the animals and the angels, and was therefore torn between the brutish and the angelic sides of his nature.

4.   Dante also felt that writing should reflect a balance between the ideas and the realities of a man's life, so we see him moving between two different aesthetic approaches in his poetry: personal realism and symbolism in allegory. Dante also challenged the accepted practice, which was to write about ideas in

Latin and more mundane matters in the vernacular language (for him, Italian). He wrote the *Comedy* in Italian.

Dante's religion told him there were three worlds in the afterlife: Hell, Purgatory, and Heaven. How does someone go about describing what no one has ever seen—life after death? Where are these places and what are they like? To answer these questions, Dante borrowed from science and, again, the religion of his day.

For Dante, both the physical and the spiritual worlds were set up as a hierarchy, leading up to God. Basically, what this means is that everything starts with God and exists in layers radiating outwards from Him.

Dante's idea of the physical universe follows the design of the astronomer Ptolemy, who taught that the earth is the center of the universe and that the following nine levels surround and rotate around the earth:

1. Moon
2. Mercury
3. Venus
4. Sun
5. Mars
6. Jupiter
7. Saturn
8. Starry Heaven
9. Crystalline Heaven (prime mobile)

Surrounding all and immobile is the Empyrean, home of God.

On the spiritual level, Dante's universe is set up so that the more God-like you are, the closer your eternal resting place will be to Him. Hell, then, is in the center of the earth, the farthest point from God. Purgatory is a mountain on the earth and Heaven is close to God.

Dante called his work simply the *Comedy;* later readers added the word divine because the work deals with God and Satan, sin and the afterlife. The Inferno is Dante-the-pilgrim's journey through Hell. The scenes he encounters there are as bizarre as anything we might see in a horror film or science fiction fantasy. There's a huge cast of characters, drawn from the Bible, from Greek mythology, and from the Italian politics of Dante's own day.

The poem is more than a supernatural travelogue, however. As you will see, it is also a journey through the human spirit, from the depths of evil to the heights of enlightenment.

THE POEM

The Plot

The story line of the *Inferno*, quite simply, is Dante's journey through Hell. He starts at the top and walks through to the bottom. The specifics, who he meets and what he sees, are discussed in the section of this guide called The Story.

If you look at the map of Dante's Hell, on page 8, you will get some idea of the major divisions and what kind of sinners are contained in each division.

On page 9 is an overview, in chart form. This overview is intended to help you keep track of where you are geographically as you go through the individual Cantos.

Reading through the overviews and looking at the map is good preparation for what you are about to read. It can also serve as a refresher in your review, reminding you of what was where.

AN OVERVIEW OF EVENTS IN THE *INFERNO*

Section of Hell and its Sinners	*Corresponding Canto(s)*
	Canto I: Dánte is Lost in the Dark Wood.
	Canto II: Virgil explains how he was sent to be Dante's guide.
Vestibule Acheron (first river of Hell)	Canto III: Dante reads the inscription over the gateway of Hell and meets Charon, the gatekeeper of Hell.
Circle I: Limbo	Cante IV: Dante visits the home of the Virtuous Pagans.

A MAP OF DANTE'S HELL

VESTIBULE: Uncommitted
Acheron
CIRCLE I: Limbo
CIRCLE II: Lustful
CIRCLE III: Gluttonous
CIRCLE IV: Hoarders and Spendthrifts
CIRCLE V: Styx Wrathful and Sullen
WALL OF DIS
CIRCLE VI: Heretics
CIRCLE VII: Phlegethon Violent against Neighbors Violent against Self Violent against God, Nature, and Art
Cliff of the Abyss
CIRCLE VIII: Malbowges i. Panderers and Seducers ii. Flatterers iii. Simoniacs iv. Sorcerers v. Barrators vi. Hypocrites vii. Thieves viii. Counselors of Fraud ix. Sowers of Discord x. Falsifiers
WALL OF GIANTS
CIRCLE IX: Cocytus Caina: Traitors to Kin Antenora: Traitors to Country Ptolomea: Traitors to Guests Judecca: Traitors to Masters SATAN

AN OVERVIEW OF EVENTS IN THE *INFERNO*

Section of Hell and its Sinners	*Corresponding Canto(s)*
Circle II: Lustful	Canto V: Dante meets two lovers, Paolo and Francesca.
Circle III: Gluttonous	Canto VI: Dante sees the Gluttonous mauled by Cerberus, the watchdog of Hell.
Circle IV: Hoarders and Spendthrifts	Canto VII: These teams of sinners roll huge rocks against each other.
River Styx Circle V: Wrathful and Sullen	Canto VIII: Phylegas ferries Dante across; Dante is accosted by a sinner.
Wall of Dis	Canto IX: The Furies threaten to show Dante and Virgil the dreaded head of Medusa; Dante and Virgil are stopped by the Fallen Angels.
Circle VI: Heretics	Canto X: Dante speaks to a Heretic in his burning coffin.
	Canto XI: Virgil explains the geography of Hell to Dante.
Circle VII: Phlegethon (river of blood)	Canto XII: Dante sees the Violent boiled in blood.
Violent against Neighbors	Canto XIII: Dante speaks with a suicide housed in a thorny tree.
Violent against Themselves	Canto XIV: The sinners writhe on the Burning Sands.
Violent against God, Nature, and Art	Canto XV: Dante's former teacher predicts Dante's future.

AN OVERVIEW OF EVENTS IN THE *INFERNO*

Section of Hell and its Sinners	Corresponding Canto(s)
Abyss	Canto XVI: Dante and Virgil search for help down the cliff.
	Canto XVII: The monster Geryon moves the poets to the Nether Hell II.
Circle VIII: Malbowges (Sins of Fraud) bowge i: Panderers and Seducers bowge ii: Flatterers	Canto XVIII: Dante sees the Panderers and Seducers whipped and the Flatterers wallowing in a trench of excrement.
bowge iii: Simoniacs	Canto XIX: The sinners suffer a perverse upside-down baptism.
bowge iv: Sorcerers	Canto XX: Dante cries over the twisted sinners and is rebuked by Virgil.
bowge v: Barrators	Canto XXI: Dante sees the Barrators plunged in boiling pitch.
	Canto: XXII: A Barrator tricks a demon-guard and causes confusion.
bowge vi: Hypocrites	Canto XXIII: Hypocrites walk in lead-lined cloaks.
bowge vii: Thieves	Canto XXIV: Dante sees a Thief reduced to ashes by an attacking snake.
	Canto XXV: The Thieves suffer strange metamorphoses.
bowge viii:	Canto XXVI: Counselors of Fraud

Section of Hell and its Sinners	Corresponding Canto(s)
Counselors of Fraud	are wrapped in sheets of flame.
	Canto XXVII: One of the sinners, Ulysses, tells his story.
bowge ix: Sowers of Discord	Canto XXVIII: Dante sees these sinners hacked apart.
bowge x: Falsifiers	Canto XXIX: The Falsifiers are stricken with hideous diseases.
	Canto XXX: Virgil rebukes Dante for enjoying a fight between two sinners.
Wall of Giants	Canto XXXI: Dante sees the Giants and is lifted into the bottom of the Pit by one of them.
Circle IX: Lake of Cocytus	Canto XXXII: The Traitors are frozen in the lake; Dante accidentally kicks one.
Traitors to Kin	
Traitors to Country	Canto XXXIII: Dante sees one sinner chewing another and hears a horrible story of treachery.
Traitors to Guests	
Traitors to Masters	Canto XXXIV: Dante sees the triple-faced Satan chewing on Judas, Cassius, and Brutus.

The Characters

Dante

Why does Dante use himself as a character? You have probably seen this form before, where a narrator will tell the story of a journey or a struggle that he took part in after the journey is finished. Joseph Conrad used it in a lot of his works. Jonathan Swift used it in *Gulliver's Travels*. What it allows is perspective. The reader gets a blow-by-blow account of the trip, with the added benefit of a narrator who has had time to think it over, analyze it, and make sense of it. The reader gets to watch the same character both as an often naive observer-participant and as an older, wiser narrator who can offer insight and meaning.

Dante has a journey to undertake in the *Divine Comedy*—he has to walk the entire universe, no less. Like the rest of us, Dante has to have a reason to start on his journey. In Canto I, he finds himself lost in the Dark Wood. And he is lost because he hasn't been paying attention to where he was going. Dante is more than physically lost. He is spiritually a soul who has wandered from the right road: Dante is a sinner, under the influence of one of the Seven Deadly Sins:

1. Pride
2. Envy
3. Wrath
4. Acedia
5. Avarice
6. Gluttony
7. Lust

Dante is guilty of the middle one, acedia. Some dictionaries give "sloth" or "laziness" as a meaning for acedia, but it is more than physical laziness. Acedia is moral laziness, inertia of the soul and will.

What is the best way to overcome laziness? Right— *do* something. Dante must compensate for his laziness by making the journey.

Through Dante's journey, we can see Dante's concept of sin. For him, all sin is basically a freezing of the will against love and grace of God. Some readers have compared this freezing of the will to an addiction, where the addict so craves his drug, his gambling, or his cigarette, that he has lost all will to stop. He also can't see—or doesn't want to see—the self-destructive path he is on.

Because Dante's specific sin is acedia, he must actively pursue the right way, the way to heaven and God. We find out as soon as Dante begins that this will not be an easy journey. It will require a DEVOUT LABOR. It won't be enough to desire the goal; he must make an effort of the will, every step along the way.

In the *Inferno*, Dante the traveler is a sleepy bumbler—not a fool exactly, but a man in need of a great deal of supervision and instruction. Why would the author use himself like this?

Dante the pilgrim is the image of every sinner struggling to understand the nature of sin, the potential for sin within the human spirit, and the result of choosing sin. In this role, we watch Dante struggle to make the physical, intellectual, and spiritual commitments necessary to complete the journey. We watch the change from an ignorant and lazy Dante in the journey to the divinely inspired (so some claim) narrator who has completed it.

Through the change, we see not only the range and complexity of the trip through Hell and sin, but the way through. If Dante can do it, so can we.

Virgil

If you were going to climb a mountain, you would probably find someone who had climbed that particular mountain before to guide you, right? It would only make sense to have someone point out the most dangerous places and tell you how he or she solved each problem along the way, rather than to attempt the climb alone, proud and blind, and then fail. For the first part of his journey, Dante needed a guide who knew something about Hell, who knew something about the epic form, and who could think differently from most. Luckily, he got the perfect guide: Virgil.

1. VIRGIL WAS A GUIDE TO THE EPIC FORM.

Historically, Virgil was a Roman poet who created a mythological beginning for the Roman Empire in his poem, the *Aeneid*. The hero of the poem, Aeneas, was a Trojan who survived the final sacking of Troy in the Trojan war by escaping with his father, his son, and some loyal men. They set off in ships to found a new Troy, which became Rome. The expedition was, like Dante's own "journey" in the *Comedy*, divinely inspired and aided (by Virgil's pagan gods). But Dante felt there was even more significance than that to Virgil's theme. The Roman Empire not only spread peace and stability; it was eventually responsible for the spread of Christianity. Although it was not biblical, Dante probably saw the *Aeneid* as a very important myth for Christians.

2. VIRGIL WAS A GUIDE WHO KNEW HELL.

In Book VI of the *Aeneid*, Aeneas travels into the underworld to speak to his father, Anchises. Dante takes many of his images of Hell from this section of the *Aeneid*. Because Virgil created the literary Hell, Dante chooses him as a guide through his Hell.

3. VIRGIL WAS A GUIDE THROUGH THE SPIRIT WORLD.

Virgil had a reputation as a "White Magician," one capable of manipulating spirits. In several places of the *Inferno*, you will see him use this power to conjure. He got this reputation from several sections of his writing which, in Dante's time, were looked at as mystical predictions from a pagan author of the coming of Christ.

4. VIRGIL STANDS FOR HUMAN REASON.

Virgil becomes in the *Inferno* the symbol of human reason. Early in the poem, Virgil tells Dante that he is there because Heaven wanted him there and that he can take Dante only part of the way. (Virgil can't enter Heaven or see God because he lacked a faith in God; he was a pagan.) Someone "more worthy" will take Dante to God. Most critics interpret this as saying that man's reason is finite, while God is infinite. Man's reason and philosophy will get him started on the right way, but the ultimate way to God is guided by a higher power.

Beatrice

Anyone hooked on romantic love stories will love the story of Beatrice. Who she was historically is not nearly as interesting as who she became for Dante, yet the two are closely connected.

In Florence, Beatrice was a member of the Portinari family, a family more wealthy and socially prominent than Dante's. Actually, Dante saw her only several times in his life. Her marriage, to a man older and richer than Dante was, like most, arranged for her. She died at age 24 in 1290.

Dante tells the story of *his* Beatrice in an earlier poem, the *Vita Nuova*. He claims that he saw her for the first time when he was nine and fell passionately in love with her. Precocious, wouldn't you say? He did not see her again until he was eighteen. (Multiples of three have mystical significance for Dante.) She smiled at him this time.

In keeping with all traditions of courtly love, Dante never actually aspired to have what we would consider a relationship with Beatrice. For him, she was the embodiment of the spiritually pure, Platonic love. Although Dante only glimpsed Beatrice several times after he was eighteen (and was betrothed and probably married himself), he claims that Beatrice inspired his very thoughts. When she died, Dante suffered a deep depression.

When she reappears in the *Divine Comedy*, she is mother, maiden, muse, and saint. She is in Heaven, top-rank, with direct communication with the Virgin Mary. It is Beatrice who sends Virgil to help Dante find his way to Heaven and to her. She doesn't appear directly in the *Inferno*, but will be his guide through Heaven and to God. What Beatrice becomes for Dante is both the Lady of courtly love and the inspiring saint of the Church, the ideal of body and soul.

This may sound incredible to us today. But Dante had a far less personal, more spiritual concept of love than we see on soap operas or read in romance novels. Instead of physical desire and passion, Dante's love was connected to spiritual perfection and the way to goodness and God. Beatrice was not an object to be loved but an inspiration to a larger love and eternal grandeur. Now that's romantic.

Other Elements

SETTING

Dante's *Inferno* deals specifically with Hell. We each have our own idea of the worst possible way to spend eternity. The differences come from differences in values, dislikes, fears, experiences, etc. When Dante created his Hell, he wanted somehow to get at all the differences and yet present a coherent pattern. Sin was sin, but the same punishment just would not do for everyone. How could he create a pattern that handled each sin uniquely and yet clearly defined sin?

1. Structurally, Hell is another one of these medieval hierarchies. Hell is a huge, tunnel-shaped pit that occupies the center of the earth directly below Jerusalem and the rest of the northern hemisphere. The pit is divided into nine circles and a vestibule (a kind of waiting room). Each circle contains souls who committed a particular kind of sin. (See the map in The Plot section of this guide.)

2. Philosophically, Hell is structured around Dante's concept of sin. Man has free will. Everyone gets, ultimately, what he chooses. As we go through Hell with Dante, we will see that the inhabitants had insisted on sin and that their punishments and suffering are very often simply a continuation of the sin they had chosen.

Dante makes distinctions between three basic kinds of sin: Incontinence (loss of self-control), Violence, and Fraud. The sins of Incontinence are the least offensive to God and, consequently, they're placed closest to him near the surface of the earth. As the sins get worse, they're placed farther from God. The sins of Fraud, the most offensive, are placed closest to the center of the earth. Satan occupies the very center of the earth.

3.   Hell is not only a geographical place, but also a representation of the potential for sin and evil within every individual human soul. As Dante travels through Hell, he sees sinners in increasingly more hideous and disgusting situations. For Dante, each situation is an image of the quality of any soul that is determined to sin in that particular way. He also suggests with his hierarchical arrangement, that the descent into sin can be a gradual process, that sinners might easily slip down into more serious sins from less serious states. (Those of you who go on to read the other parts of the *Comedy* will notice that the intensity of sin grows as we descend in Hell, but the scale of virtues climbs up Mount Purgatory and ascends to Heaven.)

Dante isn't telling us anything we don't already know. How easy is it to slip off a diet, out of an exercise routine, or a study pattern? How difficult is it to maintain enough self-discipline to keep on the path until we reach the goal? Hell is the picture of the end result of those who, spiritually, let it slide.

THEMES

Great undertakings fascinate us because they take courage: attempts to climb Mount Everest, marathon races, expeditions to the Arctic and the moon. Some poets attempt to capture the essence of a single moment or feeling in a poem. Dante, however, attempts nothing less than to present a vision of the entire universe, throughout all time and space, and the perfect pattern behind it. In this universe he places his contemporaries, historical figures, and mythological beings, defining them according to the choices they made on earth, showing them individually in situations that suggest the conditions of their souls. He also includes himself as an ignorant pilgrim trying to find himself by groping his way through and making sense of this monumental whole.

Those of us who have been told by writing teachers to "limit the topic to something manageable" are probably wondering why Dante didn't limit his topic. He does include a lot of seemingly unrelated concepts, characters, and events. He does, however, try to make clear why it is all there. One of Dante's major themes is that:

1. The whole world, ultimately, has meaning, reason, and order.

2. The source of the meaning, reason, and order is God's Divine Plan.

3. The Divine Order is both knowable and achieveable.

Thus, the way to Heaven is clearly marked, and each of us has a chance to find it—if we want.

In order to show this, Dante wanted a poem that would be not only a map of all human possibilities, but an explanation of the eternal consequences of each choice a person could make. He wanted to present the grandeur and dignity of God's creation but also all the possible ways that man may reject it. The *Inferno* is the map of the ways that God is rejected; we shouldn't forget that it is counterbalanced in the whole poem by the *Paradiso*, where God's ultimate glory really shines forth.

Dante has a monumental task—to show that the will to find God and the way to find God, are open to everyone. Some critics try to explain how Dante does this by comparing his poem to a Gothic cathedral: both have wide, sturdy bases, yet, through careful structuring, they constantly show themselves reaching for Heaven, toward God.

As we said earlier, Dante saw three parts of the universe (Hell, Purgatory, and Heaven) arranged in concentric circles. Using this structure,

1. Dante presents life on earth: lots of people and lots of choices.

2. Instead of seeing these men in their historical context, Dante puts them in order according to the eternal consequences of the lives they chose to lead.

3. The order they're placed in, and the nature of their situations within that order, give us an ethical map. (For instance, in the *Inferno*, Dante walks from the least offensive sin to the most offensive sin.)

4. From the ethical map, Dante shows us the general principles on which he believed God's plan is based.

5. Once we see the general principles, we have a way of knowing the eternal significance of any specific earthly human act.

Thus, the way to Heaven is marked, step by step.

SYMBOLISM AND ALLEGORY

Suppose you're watching a detective movie, where the "good guys" are trying to solve an ugly crime. Suddenly, you start to get a feeling that this is more than just an action-packed adventure. This crime is connected to all crimes. The "bad guys" stand for all the evil in the world. And the detective hero isn't just solving a case—he's showing us what happens when good confronts evil. That's an allegory.

An allegory is a story that has one meaning on the literal level, and another on a symbolic or metaphoric level as well. Very often in an allegory the characters represent abstract concepts. The action works out a moral, by showing how the concept "characters" interact.

Is Dante's work an allegory? How would we know? He says it is in a letter to his patron, Can Grande della Scala. (Some critics have questioned whether the document is authentic, but most recognize it as genuine.) In that letter, Dante claims he wrote the *Comedy* with *four* intended levels of meaning: narrative, allegorical, moral, and anagogical.

If we look at Dante's quest as he moves up in the hierachical structures, we can see these levels of interpretation unfold.

Level	*Movement between two poles (quest)*
Narrative	Dante makes a literal journey from *Hell* to *Heaven*.
Allegorical	Dante moves from a state of *sin* to *salvation*. Dante moves from a will frozen by acedia to an openness to the grace and love of God.
Moral	Dante moves from simple *perception* of sin and punishment to an *understanding* of what sin is, and what it does to the soul. Because he understands sin, he also comes to understand and desire the will of salvation.
Anagogical	Dante moves from the *worldly* to the *spiritual ideal*. This is the spiritual or mythical level in which Dante sees and is reunited with the One, the sublime.

Naturally, each reader must decide for himself or herself which of these levels of meaning is clear. Which meanings are important to you? For example, on the first reading, maybe only the literal level makes sense. The anagogical level we suggest is probably the most abstract and impossible to see unless you read the entire *Comedy*. The scholars who have studied Dante intensely ask us not to be intimidated by the complexity, just try to watch for it and appreciate it, like a marvelous clockwork spinning many wheels all at once.

LANGUAGE AND STYLE

The *Inferno* contains some very graphic, grotesque, and even obscene language and imagery. Sinners wallow in a river of excrement; demons pass wind to sound like bugles. Yet the poem is epic, grand—and about God. Why does Dante do this?

Historically, Dante was one of the first artists to use both low style (bawdy language, grotesque images) and high style (elevated poetic language and themes) in the same work. He was also the first to write a major epic poem in his native language, Italian, rather than in the more academically acceptable Latin.

One explanation for this is that Dante used his language and style as another way of organizing his work, to guide the reader through. Dante's mixed styles reflect the truth he is trying to present. Dante saw a connection between the mundane, street world and the elevated, spiritual world. Dante the pilgrim has to travel through the murky, disgusting depths of Hell before he can reach Heaven; so too the reader must work his or her way through physical images of sin and punishment before he or she can reach a theoretical understanding of sin's nature and the divine order that gives each his eternal place. In other words,

Dante uses a mixture of language styles to lead the reader to his more abstract meanings and themes.

It may be difficult, when you're reading a translation, to get all the nuances of style that Dante included. Also, it's hard for us in the 20th century to remember that this language seemed shocking or slangy in the 14th century, because it's completely acceptable in literature today. Keep reminding yourself, though, that Dante was one of the pioneers in using "street" language in literature.

Also, Dante's style reflects his interest in polarities. Two extremes of language—coarse and refined—continually pull the reader in different directions. A formal "high style" of writing is polarized with a casual, colloquial "low style." Partly, this creates the variety that is important to Dante, to show how many possibilities there are in his quest. It also exerts a tension that keeps the poem moving, never resting with one level of meaning—just as Dante the pilgrim can never rest until his quest is finished.

FORM

The form of the *Inferno* derives from the fact that it is a comedy and an epic and involves a quest.

1. THE COMEDY

From what you have read so far, you can see that the *Inferno* is not all that funny and are probably wondering why it is part of the *Divine Comedy*. We think of comedy in terms of TV situation comedies where a problem situation is presented in the first few minutes of the program and is resolved by the end of the episode. Actually, comedy as a form has a successful ending. The hero of a dramatic comedy wants something and certain people and/or elements are stopping him from getting it. The Canadian literary critic Nor-

throp Frye says that the obstacles to a hero's goals
make up the action of the comedy; overcoming the
obstacles is the comic resolution. The *Divine Comedy* is
about Dante's attempt to get to Heaven, to Beatrice,
and to God. Because he is successful at overcoming
the obstacles within himself and the obstacles along
his way, the poem is called the *Comedy*.

2. THE EPIC

Some of you have read epic poems; perhaps the
Iliad, the *Odyssey*, or *Beowulf*. From them you know
the basic points of definition. An epic is a long narrative poem of grand scale involving superhuman heros
upon whom the nation or even the world depends.
An epic usually is written in elevated or very formal
language, has an invocation of the Muses, and begins
in medias res, in the middle of the action. Is the *Divine
Comedy* an epic?

In the broader application of the term, it is. It does
begin in medias res, but is not always written in elevated language. (See the preceding section on Dante's
language and style.) The scale of the poem is clearly
epic, since it includes the entire universe. The hero,
though he does accomplish his challenging task, cannot be superhuman and still convey Dante's major
theme that God and Heaven are accessible to all of us.
Whether the world depends on Dante or not becomes
an issue on this thematic level. On a literal level, Dante's success or failure won't affect anyone. But on a
metaphoric or allegorical level, Dante's successful
journey points the way to Heaven for the rest of mankind. Whether we decide the *Divine Comedy* is an epic
or not, the poem does have epic characteristics.

3. THE QUEST

The motif of a mythical hero's quest is familiar to
many of you. The hero becomes separated from the
people and/or the place of his birth, becomes aware of

a need or a problem, takes a dangerous journey to an unknown place to win either a prize or knowledge to help him resolve the problem, and returns to save the people. The *Aeneid* and the *Odyssey* are based on a hero's quest.

Dante the character is a questing pilgrim, lost and eager to find the way to salvation and to Heaven. He becomes separated, lost in the Dark Wood, and journeys through the entire universe. From what, you ask, does he save the world? What huge contribution does he make? Again, on the literal level, none. On other levels of meaning, however, he brings back the understanding and the inspiration that make it possible for him to be the author of the *Divine Comedy* and to show people the way to heaven. How Dante does this is more clearly explained above in the section on symbolism and allegory.

STRUCTURE

The numbers three, nine, and ten recur often in the *Divine Comedy* and have special significance.

- There are 3 parts to the *Comedy:* Inferno, Purgatorio, and Paradiso.
- There are 33 cantos (verse chapters) in each part.
- Including one canto of introduction, there are 100 cantos altogether.
- Each canto is written in terza rima, stanzas of three lines with the first and third lines rhyming and the second line rhyming with the first line of the next stanza.
- There are 3 basic kinds of sin: Incontinence, Violence, and Fraud.
- There are nine circles of Hell, with the Vestibule making 10 levels. (Purgatory and Heaven are subdivided in much the same numerical way.)

The numbers are another way Dante creates significance or meaning. Three is the number of the Trinity—Father, Son, and Holy Spirit. Nine is the square of three. Adding one for the unity of the Trinity gives ten, considered a "perfect" number in medieval thinking. One hundred is the square of ten. Dante, writing of God, perfection, and the ideal unity of the universe, structures his poem around these numbers. This may seem like an elaborate, artificial game to you, but it wasn't for Dante. These numbers had mystical significance. And because Dante was writing about God's complex design, he wanted to make his poem have an appropriately complex design to match.

The Story

Canto I

Most epic poems begin in medias res, in the middle of things, and the *Inferno* is no exception. As a matter of fact, Dante is in the middle of several things. One, he finds himself in the middle of the Dark Wood—lost. Second, he is in the middle of his life, "Midway this way of life. . ." This much he tells us before it becomes clear that he's not just "lost" in any simple ordinary sense. He turns to go back the way he came, up a mountain, but his way is blocked by three animals: a leopard, a lion, and a she-wolf. He flees from the animals back down the mountain and comes across the shade of Virgil who offers to take him by another path.

Animals? The ghost of a Roman poet? Where is

Dante that he can't go back the way he came? Why does Virgil, of all possible people, happen to be there? Looking back for evidence, we find that Dante gives us one more clue. He tells us the reason why he was lost: he was drowsy and inattentive.

We can put it all together this way. Dante is lost in his quest for salvation. He has strayed from the "right road" because of his sin, acedia, or moral laziness. Because he has not been attentive to the active pursuit of good, he has lost the way. He can't go back the way he came because that is the way of sin. He is in the middle of a moral mess. Virgil is there to help Dante find his way out.

NOTE: The critics have many explanations for the animals. Some think that the animals represent the three kinds of sin: the leopard representing the sins of incontinence, the lion the sins of violence, and the she-wolf the sins of fraud. Still other critics think that the beasts represent the sins of pleasure, ambition, and greed, respectively. Others see the beasts as symbolic of the forces at work in the political world of Dante: the leopard representing Florentine politics, the lion representing the French desire to rule in Italy, and the she-wolf representing the Papacy and its involvement in political affairs. Whatever meaning is true (and it could be all of them), the animals stand in Dante's way and Virgil is there to help.

Canto II

The sun is setting on this Good Friday evening and Dante, after a brief time with Virgil, begins to lose heart. He tells Virgil that he is neither Virgil's far-journeying hero, nor St. Paul, the converted disciple who travelled widely, spreading Christ's teachings. Virgil tells Dante quite frankly that he is a coward and that he should be aware of the special notice he is being given in Heaven. Dante learns that Beatrice visited Virgil in Hell and asked him, tearfully, to help Dante find his way, and she did so at the prompting of St. Lucy and the Virgin herself. Spurred by the tale of Beatrice's goodness and tears on his behalf, Dante resumes his journey with zest and feelings of dedication.

It is not an accident that Dante is making his journey on the weekend before Easter. Christ died on Good Friday and was buried until his resurrection on Easter Sunday. During that time, he is said to have descended into Hell and Purgatory. Christ's resurrection freed sinners from eternal condemnation; to be freed from his own sin, sloth, Dante too must descend through sin and understand its nature and its effects on the soul. In this, we see the beginnings of one of Dante's themes, the necessity for all those who wish salvation to make a like journey.

The Virgin Mary, who gave birth to God in Christ, is often seen as the symbol of Divine Grace, the power granted by God that directs the soul on its quest. St. Lucy is the patron saint of all those with weak sight. Beatrice is Dante's special inspiration. He may not feel worthy of her attention, but when this ideal of body and soul beckons, how can Dante refuse?

Canto III

"Lay down all hope, you that go in by me." So goes the last line of the ominous message over the lintel of the gateway to Hell. Dante's reaction is as you'd expect: he is terrified. The message serves to set the tone of seriousness for the quest, and to make it clear that Dante's journey, despite the helpers and the guides, will be a dangerous one. If it weren't, would anyone want to read about it?

The entire message of the lintel, too, begins to tell what Dante the pilgrim must learn on his journey. Hell was made by the power, the wisdom, and the love of God. This probably sounds paradoxical. If we keep in mind, however, that God created man with *free will*, we see Hell has to exist to give people a choice with that free will. Men are free to turn away from love and wisdom; they are free to be satisfied with less than eternal enlightenment and happiness. Hell is that choice. The message is clearly written over the doorway. Dante will not understand the message in this way until he has made the journey through. Possibly we, too, will come back at the end of our reading to see a clearer, richer meaning in the lintel's message.

And so the poets enter Hell. Dante's senses are assaulted. The sights and sounds of confusion, disharmony, and lack of dignity and distinction astound him. He begs Virgil to identify these wretched souls who run, tormented by swarms of hornets and wasps. Virgil tells Dante that these are the souls of the Opportunists, those who, on earth, could not take a stand on any issue. Here, too, are the angels who did not fight with either Michael (God's general) or with Lucifer (the rebel Satan) in the battle of Heaven. Hell does not want to claim these souls or to confuse them with those who made a choice, even if it was the wrong choice. Heaven would not sully itself. And so those who would not choose in life are goaded forever in this Vestibule of Hell.

Looking ahead, Dante sees the bank of a wide stream crowded with souls eager to cross. This is the river Acheron, the first river in Hell. The name Acheron and the boatman who is ferrying his way across, Charon, come from Greek mythology. Charon, old and shaggy, his eyes rimmed with fire, screams at Dante and Virgil that Dante will have to find another way across the river: Charon's skiff will not bear the weight of a living soul. The sound of Charon's bawlings and the sight of the multitude of shades sliding down the banks, and cursing all it is possible to curse, combine with the shock of a slight earthquake to undo Dante. He faints.

NOTE: In a first reading of any poem, a reader is generally looking for a sense of the meaning and not studying such subtleties as the kind of language and sentence structure that a poet uses. Dante's style and language are such a large part of his structure, meaning, and themes, however, that even a beginning reader will want to give it some attention.

Hell is ugly. Dante makes us feel the ugliness with the imagery that appeals to all our senses. In this canto, Dante emphasizes the volume and the dissonance of the shrieks of the sinners goaded by the wasps. We see the sinners sliding down the muddy banks; we hear them screaming curses. We feel the thud of Charon's oars on the backs of the lingerers. The final sensory outrage is the shaking of the earth.

Different translations will vary, but most translations of this canto have many inverted sentences and are filled with harsh, guttural words. Read the passages about Charon out loud. Is it hard to read? Is it fluid or choppy?

Dante makes his language create his meaning. When Dante wants to describe a particularly grotesque aspect, his language will match his subject. Look for a continuation of this in other places.

Canto IV

Dante awakens from his swoon near the edge of the actual pit of Hell. Together, he and Virgil enter the First Circle, Limbo. Dante is somewhat disturbed to hear that all those born before Christ, including Virgil, are assigned to this place. He questions Virgil closely on this point and discovers that when Christ descended into Hell after his crucifixion, He did take such men as Noah, Moses, David, and Abraham with Him to Heaven. But since that time, no one has changed position.

In the middle of this conversation, a voice hails the return of Virgil. Virgil presents to Dante the shades of the classical writers Homer, Horace, Ovid, and Lucan, and Dante is pleased to be a sixth in the presence of such great minds. Dante also sees the resting shades of Socrates, Plato, Ptolemy, and many others.

NOTE: Why are such notable people in Hell? It hardly seems fair that they should be here simply because they were born before Christ. We can better understand Limbo if we remember, again, the many levels of meaning in the *Inferno*. On an allegorical level, the sinners cease to be important as historical figures and instead become representations of various conditions of the human spirit.

Limbo is not a place of torment. It resembles the Elysian Fields of Virgil's *Aeneid* where Aeneas meets his father. The Virtuous Pagans housed here are certainly not evil. What failings they have are the failings of human reason alone. In other words, these shades represent the condition of the spirit that lacks faith; the failure of such a spirit is the failure to imagine better.

Another thing we should notice before going on is the mild rebuke that Virgil gives Dante. Virgil reminds Dante that he has not asked for an identification of the shades. This will not be the last time that Dante gets in trouble for such negligence. Is Virgil just being a nag?

Dante's physical journey through Hell is only part of his journey; he is also journeying, allegorically, through the depths of the potential evil within the soul. It will not be enough for him to see where and how each sin is punished. He must understand what each sin did to the soul, how it twisted the spirit away from God. To understand the whole concept of sin, he must understand each particular along the way. Virgil must point out each hurdle or lapse in the moral and allegorical journeys just as he points out the geographical difficulties of the literal journey. So, like a good teacher, he nags a bit.

Canto V

Everyone loves the story of forbidden love, including Dante (who, remember, was denied even a private conversation with his Beatrice). Giving in to the wrong love is Dante's idea of the least offensive sin. Once inside of Hell, the Lustful are the first sinners that Dante sees.

Virgil and Dante descend to the Second Circle and encounter Minos, the judge of Hell. Minos wraps his tail around himself, as many coils as the number of descents each shade is to make, while the shade pours out a confession of all his wrongs. When Minos sees Dante, he screams that they should not be deceived by the wide open door and refuses to let them pass. Virgil quiets Minos by telling him his hindrance is in vain, and then he leads Dante past Minos to view the

sinners guilty of Lust, the first of the sins of incontinence.

Those shades are swept around on a whirlwind,
driven and wailing. As they whip past the poets, Virgil points out the shades of the famous lovers: Cleo-
patra, Helen, Paris, and Tristan among others. Dante,
although stunned by the sights and sounds, asks to
speak to two shades who ride the winds holding
hands, Paolo and Francesca da Rimini. How did they
come to be caught in this whirlwind?

NOTE: Dante's readers would have been familiar
with this story. Francesca was the wife of Paolo's
brother, Gianciotto. This marriage, like many of that
day, was a political union not a love match; Gianciotto
was as deformed as Paolo was beautiful. All that Francesca tells Dante is how she and her brother-in-law fell
in love. In innocence, Paolo and Francesca spent one
afternoon reading the romance of Lancelot and Guinevere. Their eyes met, they kissed, and "they read no
more that day." Francesca's story so moves the
tender-hearted Dante that he faints.

No other canto of the entire *Comedy* has inspired
such attention and artistic interpretation as this canto
has. The lovers' story is very beautiful and very sad.
Why are they in Hell? They died when Gianciotto
found the lovers together and stabbed them both. Yet
their love and the passion are so understandable—is
the punishment fair?

Francesca is not punished so much for the act as for
the failing. She fails a larger kind of love. In Hell, she
is bound forever to a shade without possibility of
growth or change. She could have chosen the love
which leads to God and forms eternal bonds with glo-

ry and perfection. But her love for Paolo's beauty blinded her to the possibility of choosing God's love.

We should also look carefully at the excuse that Francesca offers. It is naive but believeable. In this first circle of sin, it represents the first consent of the soul to sin. It is easy, human, almost forgiveable. Perhaps Dante is trying to demonstrate how easy the first step into sin is. We are aware of the consequences of the lovers' choice. But if we hadn't seen them in Hell, we might not understand this step as a sin, as a weakness of will, as a wrong choice of brief passion over eternal glory.

Canto VI

Dante awakens from his faint to a cold, ceaseless rain and an earth that smells of rot and decay. He is in the Third Circle where the Gluttonous wallow in the drenched earth and are mauled by the vile, triple-headed Cerberus, traditional guardian of Hell. The shades squirm, scream, and writhe to escape the inescapable monster, who also threatens Dante and Virgil. Virgil picks up handfuls of the slime and throws them in the mouths of Cerberus, and the poets hurry past.

Dante speaks to a fellow Florentine who has been nicknamed Ciacco, which means "pig." Ciacco tells Dante of some of the events that are to happen in Florence before Virgil moves Dante along. While they travel on, Dante asks Virgil whether the suffering he has encountered will grow more intense or will lessen after the Judgment Day. Virgil replies that the souls will become "more perfect," which is usually explained as a belief that the souls will be united to their bodies at that time.

NOTE: Most readers find Francesca and Paolo sad and Ciacco rather repulsive. The sin has moved from one of mutual indulgence to solitary self-indulgence; the image of the soul has moved from one buffeted by passion to one alone and groveling. The use of Cerberus reinforces the image of the uncontrolled appetite that is common to all the sins of incontinence.

Canto VII

At the entrance of the Fourth Circle, Virgil and Dante are threatened by Pluto, mythological god of the underworld. Much as he did with Minos and the other figures who challenge their passage, Virgil quickly shuts up the beast with a word about the nature of their quest. In this circle, Dante sees two groups of sinners rolling huge rocks against each other, turning and wheeling back again. These opposing groups are the Hoarders and the Spendthrifts, who are by definition incompatible with each other and full of mutual antagonism. The sight prompts Dante to ask Virgil about Luck, and Virgil takes the time to explain some aspects of divine providence to Dante.

The poets come upon the second of the rivers in Hell, the river Styx. Dante sees mud-stained and discontented shades in the river. They are beating and tearing at each other with fists, heads, bodies, and all. Virgil explains that these are the souls of the Wrathful, those who could not control their anger. Under the surface of the river lie the Sullen; their sulky murmurs of anger bubble to the top.

This Fourth Circle contains the last of the sins of Incontinence. The image of the Hoarders and Spendthrifts demonstrates how futile such irrational appe-

tites are. In the group of the Wrathful, we can see how
the sins of incontinence have defiled the soul. When
we move from a vision of Paolo and Francesca, mutu-
ally sharing their sin and fate, to the Wrathful who
furiously lust to inflict pain on each other, we see the
instability and the repulsiveness of the decline into
sin.

It is from this literal and allegorical point of view
that Dante and Virgil see the walls that surround the
Nether Hell, the city of Dis.

Canto VIII

Picture Dante and Virgil walking along the murky
marsh of the river Styx until they can see the gate to
the fiery walls which surround the city of Dis, the
beginning of the Nether (Lower) Hell I. A signal light
comes from the top of the tower and a boatman sets
forth across the river to fetch Dante and Virgil. Phylegas, who in Greek mythology set fire to Apollo's
temple, is the boatman. He fumes at the knowledge
that Virgil and Dante are not sinners who have come
for placement, but he does ferry them across.

The boat, precariously positioned because of Dante's weight, sets out across the grimy water. A head
appears in the mud and challenges Dante's passage
"before his time." Dante recognizes the shade as Filippo Argenti, a fellow Florentine. When Dante tells
Filippo to remain and rot in the slime, Filippo grabs
the boat. Virgil casts him off and turns to embrace
Dante with a most unusual blessing: "Blessed is the
womb that bore thee." Dante wishes that he could see
Filippo at the hands of some of the Wrathful. While
the poets watch, Filippo is beaten and mauled by a
gang of fellow sinners.

This can be a very confusing passage. It looks like Virgil is encouraging Dante to be cruel and un-Christian. The line he chooses comes from Christ himself and suggests that Dante's reaction has brought him closer to his goal. This is the first time that Dante has not pitied the sinners; it is the first time he was repulsed by them. Allegorically, Dante sees for the first time how vile and degrading sin, in the image of the sinner, really is. For this step, Dante is rewarded. Immediately after this episode, however, Dante's quest gets very difficult.

The poets draw near to the gate of the city of Dis and Dante loses heart. Phylegas lets them off near the gate where they are met by some of the Fallen Angels, those that fought with Lucifer in the battle of Heaven. They challenge Dante and refuse him passage while he is still alive. They also tell Virgil to let Dante find the way back himself. When he hears this, Dante begs Virgil to quit and to allow them to go back together, quickly. Virgil tells Dante to take heart—their passage is guaranteed from above, and Virgil will not abandon him. Virgil does, however, leave Dante for a brief private meeting with the Fallen Angels. While Dante quivers in fear, he sees the gate slammed in Virgil's face. Virgil returns to Dante with assurances that they will win entry and that help is on the way.

NOTE: You are probably wondering why the entrance to Dis is so impassable. What is the significance of the Fallen Angels? What threat do they pose? On one level, it makes a good story. Another way to look at it comes from its juxtaposition with the reward Dante has just received from Virgil.

Dante is just beginning to understand the nature of sin and how it blinds the soul and binds the will. Virgil is Dante's teacher and guide, a provider of light. The Fallen Angels, in their attempts to separate Virgil and Dante, are deniers of light, if you will. They represent the loss of reason that is part of the will to sin. Had the Fallen Angels been successful in separating Virgil and Dante, this would have been the end of the guidance of reason, and Dante, literally and figuratively, would have been lost.

Virgil's faltering in this situation suggests that humanism alone, represented by Virgil, often underestimates the power of evil and is confused by the will to evil. The Nether Hell gate is the passage point from the sins of Incontinence to the sins of Violence. To deal with this more potent sin, help from a source higher than reason, namely Heaven, must intercede.

Canto IX

Dante is very confused by Virgil's rejection at the gates of Dis and asks, tactfully, whether Virgil actually knows what he is doing. Virgil assures Dante that he has made the trip before. Dante loses track of what Virgil is saying when he sees above him the horrible shades of the Furies. The Furies, or the Erinyes, were, in Greek mythology, the avenging goddesses who haunted and tormented those who had committed great crimes, particularly murder in the family. The sight of the snake-haired beasts and the sounds of their shrieking make Dante clutch Virgil in fright. They scream, "Fetch Medusa," the legendary Gorgon whose face turns men to stone. Because Dante is still alive, he could literally be petrified by this sight. Virgil cries instructions to Dante; he should turn and cover

his eyes. Not trusting Dante, Virgil places his own
hands over Dante's hands and eyes.

Thus blinded momentarily, Dante hears and feels
what seems to be an earthquake. Virgil bids him to
look across the marsh. Through the mist, Dante sees a
Messenger of Heaven coming forward. The angry
messenger reaches the gate, opens it with a touch and
chastises the Fallen Angels for trying to prevent what
has already been ordained in Heaven. The messenger
leaves without speaking to Virgil or Dante. The poets
enter the gate and find themselves in a strange cemetery. The tombstones are all upturned, and the
graves are filled with fire.

NOTE: Again, reason, in the figure of Virgil, is
not enough to fulfill Dante's quest. As the two poets
pass through this gate, they are entering a deeper,
more powerful realm of sin. The sinners in the Nether
Hell are not those souls who have a weak will, little
self-control, or a limited vision. The souls here have
actively chosen sin. They are violent and threatening
to Dante because that is the condition of the spirit of
one who chooses violence, destruction, and perversion. Dante must see this condition of the spirit for
what it is if he is ever to fully understand sin, thus
saving himself from it. Virgil is uncertain, so, it will
take everything Dante's got to make it through.

Most critics agree that the Furies are the image of
fruitless remorse that does not lead to repentance.
Medusa can be seen as the power of the irrational,
which can freeze the free will and even separate the
will from reason. She can also be seen as the image of
the despair which hardens the heart, making repentance impossible. Literally and symbolically, these are
formidable adversaries.

The Divine Messenger steps in to assist reason (Virgil) in the face of the irrational in much the same way that Virgil helps Dante physically and intellectually in the places that are tough going. Students should notice here that those inspired by Heaven—Virgil, Beatrice, the Messenger—are very ready to assist Dante's quest, while the sinners and those who are the images of sin only inhibit Dante's progress and do damage to each other. This motif will become even clearer as Dante descends farther into Hell.

Canto X

The cemetery in which Dante and Virgil find themselves is the Sixth Circle of Hell, the home of the Heretics. Dante is hailed by Farinata degli Uberti, a Florentine who was hated by Dante's ancestors for his part in a particularly brutal ambush. Dante is frightened to hear himself beckoned from one of these tombs and clings to Virgil, who turns him around to talk to the shade. Before the conversation has gone very far, another shade rises to a sitting position in the same tomb to ask about his son. This is Cavalcante dei Cavalcanti whose son, Guido, was Farinata's son-in-law, and a poet-friend of Dante. Dante refers to Guido in the past tense, and Cavalcante, misunderstanding Dante's response, thinks his son is dead. At this, he swoons back into the tomb. As if he were not interrupted at all, Farinata continues to justify his actions to Dante. Dante leaves the pair with a message for Cavalcante that his son is still alive and sets off again with Virgil, for it is getting late.

NOTE: You are probably wondering why Dante has included such details as Florentine politics and parental devotion in this canto, or in the whole poem for that matter. Dante, over and over, is trying to show that the pain of Hell is the pain of the particular sin that was chosen. Both Farinata and Cavalcante are specific manifestations of a larger sin; they are both heretics.

For Dante, heresy was intellectual stubbornness. These sinners knew what the Church taught but preferred their own interpretation. They did not trust what should or could be trusted. Both men continue in Hell to pursue, blindly and stubbornly, their own limited visions. By putting these seemingly unconnected men and conversations together in one tomb, Dante demonstrates the self-centered pride and isolation of heresy.

Note, too, how the punishment fits the sin. The unbending pride is housed in an unyielding iron tomb; the contempt for the right way is punished in scathing flames.

Canto XI

When Dante and Virgil reach the brink of the Seventh Circle, the stink so overpowers Dante that he falls behind a rock for relief. Virgil takes this recess time to explain the structure of Hell. Because of the allegorical nature of the poems structure, the geography lesson will also be an ethics lesson.

Dante's concept of ethics comes primarily from the Greek philosopher Aristotle who saw three types of wrong behavior: uncontrolled appetite (Incontinence); perverted appetite (Bestiality); and the abuse of human faculties, especially that of reason (Malice). Dante blends these classical ethical categories with the specifically Christian sins of nonbelief (paganism) and wrong-belief (heresy) to devise his scheme of the pit.

Canto XII

Virgil and Dante have walked to the edge of the plain housing the tombs of the Heretics. They find themselves facing a sheer precipice. Virgil leads Dante to a place where a large pile of rocks makes the precipice passable. At this point, they encounter the Minotaur, half man and half bull, and must find a way past him. Virgil taunts the monster with a reference to Theseus who, in the Greek legends, slew him in the upper world. The poets take advantage of the monster's raging fury to slip past him down the rocks to the edge of Phlegethon, the river of boiling blood. This is Circle Seven, where the Violent are punished. Phlegethon boils those who were Violent against their neighbors.

Before they even step off the rocks, Dante and Virgil are challenged by the guardians of the river, the centaurs, who are half horse and half man. The centaur Chiron, the legendary tutor of such Greek heroes as Achilles and Theseus, speaks to the poets and asks if, indeed, Dante is still living. Chiron employs Nessus, the centaur who fell in love with Hercules' wife and tricked her into poisoning Hercules, to carry Virgil and Dante across the river.

Virgil points out to Dante that the river is not of the same depth all around. In the deeper part, those who committed their lives to violence—the conqueror Alexander the Great, the Greek god of frenzied revelry Dionysius—are boiled. Those who were less violent are boiled to a lesser degree, as the river is only ankle deep in some parts. It is at this point that Nessus tells the poets to cross.

NOTE: What do the two kinds of mythological monsters in this canto have in common? Each is a compound of man and beast. The Minotaur is part man and part bull; the centaurs are part horse and part man. As guardians to the first circle of the sins of violence, they suggest to us that such sins spring from the perversion of the human spirit, to the point that animal passions outdo human reason. In the myth, the Minotaur was the product of lust, pride, and deceit. Annually he devoured the sacrifice of seven boys and seven girls until he was defeated by Theseus. Here, the monster cannot do his job because he is caught in a blind rage. These monsters reinforce the transition from the sins of incontinence, loss of control, to the sins of violence, the lust for destruction.

Canto XIII

In our day and age, suicide is sometimes viewed as romantic. You therefore may have to adjust your thinking to Dante's in this canto about the Suicides. Modern readers, who understand suicide as a psychological symptom, often have a hard time with the harsh punishment that Dante inflicts upon these sinners. Before judging him harshly, try to see this sin and punishment in terms of his total concept.

Once Nessus has departed, Dante and Virgil walk into a forest of dry, thorny trees. The ugly, shrieking Harpies sit on these trees.

NOTE: The Harpies, the bird-women guardians of the Wood of the Suicides, are another example of the half-human, half-beast monster from mythology that Dante chooses as the image of the sins of Violence. In Virgil's *Aeneid*, the Harpies attack Aeneas and his men when they land on the Strophades, stealing and defiling their food. Thus, as the image of the will to destroy, they guard and torment the souls of those who denied and rejected life on earth.

The poets hear a wailing but Dante can't see anyone who might be making the sound. Virgil bids Dante to break off a branch from one of these trees. Dante does as he is told and is terrorized by the result. Blood and words pour from the place where he has plucked the branchlet. The tree asks Dante why he has torn away its bones.

Virgil answers for the stricken Dante. He begs forgiveness from the wounded soul, explaining that he asked Dante to tear away a branch in order to see for himself what he might not have believed if he were simply told. Virgil also tells the soul that if he speaks with Dante, Dante might be able to explain his sin when he returns to earth.

This is the Wood of the Suicides. The tree-embedded soul is Pier delle Vigne, once counselor to Frederick II. Accused of treason and conspiracy, he tells Dante, he took his own life rather than live with shame. The shade goes on to tell Dante how the souls of the Suicides come to be in the leafless trees. When a soul is forced from its body in the violence of suicide, Minos sends it down to the Seventh Circle. The soul, wherever it lands, falls into the ground, sprouts, and grows into a sapling and then a tree. The Harpies feed on the leaves and branches, causing great pain. After the Judgment Day, when all sinners' bodies are reunited with their souls, the bodies of the Suicides will hang from the thorns of the trees.

As Dante and Virgil wait for more words from the Suicide, they hear the crashing sounds of a hunt. Two naked shades come running toward them, chased by a pack of black dogs.

These are the Profligates, those who squandered the source of their sustenance in life. It makes sense that they share the same ring as the Suicides: both denied themselves the life they were intended. These

Profligates are different from the Spendthrifts in Circle Four. The Profligates willfully destroyed the social order that provides for the continuation of life; the Spendthrifts are guilty of simple extravagance. For example, Jacomo, the soul who was torn apart by the ravaging bitches, had a habit of burning down the houses of his workers for the fun of it. Today, rock groups who smash their instruments on stage and wreck their hotel rooms would certainly end up here; they aren't just extravagant, they're willfully destructive.

One of the Profligate shades, Jacomo of Saint Andrea, tries to take refuge in a thick bush, but the pursuers tear into the bush and grab the sinner, ripping him apart and carrying away the pieces. The Suicide embodied in that bush has been inadvertently wounded; he yells questions of "Why me?" after the pack. This Suicide, who tells Dante and Virgil only that he is Florentine and has hanged himself, begs the poets to gather the scattered leaves and branches near the base of his bush before leaving.

Try to see Dante's image of sin and his concept of Divine Order in the image he has chosen for the Suicides. Again, Dante feels that sin is chosen with free will; eternal placement is simply a continuation of whatever was chosen during life. Suicides chose to separate body from soul and are, thus, eternally separated, even when other shades will regain their bodies. They chose a violent separation and are continually preyed upon by the violent Harpies. They chose to defile a form given by God and are continually defiled in form. They denied the purpose of Christ's crucifixion, and their bodies will be crucified forever. One thing that cannot be denied, however, is the eternal life of the spirit. Just as Dante must make this arduous journey because his laziness has threatened his eternal life, so the Suicides must continue to live, are forced to sprout and grow branches. This spiritual life cannot be denied. Man is free only to choose its form.

You may still think that Dante is cruel to those whom life has treated cruelly enough, but you have to admit that he is consistent in his application. You will see, too, that Dante puts his friends as well as his enemies in Hell. (One is coming up in Canto XV.) Apparently he doesn't want to put his own feelings before the Divine Order.

Canto XIV

Dante and Virgil gather the leaves and branches of the nameless Suicide before finding their way to the edge of the wood. Here they find a wide moat of sand on which herds of souls lie flat or hunched. All of them writhe, trying to avoid great sheets of flame that fall continually on the sand. Dante questions Virgil about the place and is answered vehemently by Capaneus who, in the war against Thebes, boasted that not even Jove could stop him. Virgil warns Capaneus that, since he won't quiet his blasphemy, he will suffer even more.

Careful not to step onto the Burning Sands, the poets walk at the edge until they come to a horrible, bubbling red brook with banks of stone. Virgil explains the source of this stream and its path. Dante asks questions about the sources and paths of all the rivers in Hell, which pleases Virgil. He explains some and tells Dante that he will shortly see the rest for himself. They head for a safe crossing place across the Burning Sands.

NOTE: The river Phlegethon, the Wood of the Suicides, and the Burning Sands are all part of the punishment for the various ways that man can be violent. The sands are sterile, as were the trees of the Suicides. Those that are violent against God, Nature, and Art make sterile what should be fruitful. The wrath of the flames of fire are reminiscent of the wrath shown by God in the destruction of Sodom and Gomorrah.

Canto XV

Walking across the dike that crosses Phlegethon, Dante and Virgil see a group of shades running past, taking careful note of them and of each other. These are the Sodomites, the sexually unnatural. One of the pack recognizes Dante and puts his hand out to him. Dante peers at the burned and scarred shade and recognizes Brunetto Latini, a Florentine scholar and author. Brunetto asks Dante how he happened to be there and tells him that, if he had not died so soon, he would have helped Dante achieve his fame. Brunetto also prophesies ill for Dante: "For thy good deeds will be thine enemy." Dante tells Brunetto that his fatherly image and his teachings remain with Dante still. Then Brunetto has to return to the perpetual running to which he is condemned.

Brunetto was Dante's intellectual mentor. His books embodied medieval philosophy and intellectual order. It is obvious from this canto that Dante had a great deal of affection and respect for him. Dante put not only his enemies in Hell, but also any of his friends whom he felt God would condemn. He wouldn't put his own judgment against the principles of God's judgment, but at the same time he wouldn't downplay or reject the sincere respect he held for valuable contributions that may pass between men.

The perpetual running of the shades here parallels the drifting of the Lustful in Canto V. The Sodomites are violent against nature, according to Dante, and have perverted the natural powers of the body. They must run after that which they have denied. Many of you may have objections to Dante's feeling of sin here; it's good to keep in mind the values of the time when it was written.

Canto XVI

Dante and Virgil continue along the rock path over Phlegethon until they are within earshot of where the river runs over a huge cliff. Before they reach the edge, Dante sees and speaks to several well-known Florentine politicians. The men can't stop the incessant running to which they are condemned so they form themselves into a wheel, each watching Dante very carefully while they speak. The men ask particulars of Florence; Dante gives them a depressing report.

When they have finished talking, Dante and Virgil proceed to the edge of the cliff. Virgil asks Dante to take off the rope belt that he is wearing. Dante promptly does so, telling the reader that at one point he had hoped to catch the leopard with it. Virgil throws the girdle over the cliff. Dante thinks to himself that some strange creature will probably appear out of the depths in response to this signal. Virgil, apparently reading Dante's thoughts, replies that that is exactly what is to happen. Dante begs the reader to believe what he scarcely could, that out of the mists appeared the head of some strange beast.

NOTE: There are many interpretations of the source and purpose of the rope and its use as a signal. Dante does say that he hoped to catch the leopard with it; perhaps we can see this as a step in Dante's allegorical journey. The sins of Incontinence, symbolized by the leopard, are left behind and Dante's defenses against them are freed for other uses.

Canto XVII

Dante would have made great movies because he had a wonderful sense of visual drama. As Virgil and Dante stand near the edge of the cliff, the monster Geryon comes up over the edge in response to Virgil's signal. In Greek mythology, this monster had three heads and a human form. Here, however, he has the face of a benign man, the claws of a beast, and the tail of a reptile. His multifaceted and deceptive form make him a perfect image of Fraud, which is the corruption of appetite, will, and intellect.

While Virgil negotiates passage down the cliff with Geryon, he sends Dante to view a group of shades that sit on the edge of the Burning Sands, the Usurers. These sinners flap their arms, gesturing to keep away from the burning flames that sweep over them. Around each neck is a purse. It may seem odd to a reader that the Usurers share the same ring as the Sodomites, until Dante's feeling about making use of God's gifts of nature becomes clear. The Suicides refused life; the Profligates refused to honor the materials that sustain life; the Sodomites make sterile what is supposed to be fertile (the human body); the Usurers make fertile what is supposed to be sterile— money. To live from the labors of others, and to have luxuries at the expense of their basic needs, is their sin. (When you finish paying your student loans, you might try creating your own punishment for the Usurers.)

When Dante returns to Virgil, Virgil tells Dante to grab hold of Geryon's shoulders, and he will transport the pair down to the next circle. Dante makes a show of his bravery but implores Virgil to grab hold of him for safety. Virgil does so, telling Dante he will sit behind him to prevent Dante from suffering any mischief from the monster's tail. Geryon turns, descends the cliff, and shakes off the poets at the bottom.

NOTE: If you will remember Dante's difficulty getting through the gates of Dis, you might see some parallels here. Going through the gates meant passage from the first kind of sin, Incontinence, to a more serious kind, Violence. The steep walls of the Abyss represent passage from the sins of Violence to the most offensive kind of sin, Fraud. It seems that when the poets make a change of such significance, even Virgil has to get some assistance. Keep your eyes open for one more place where this is so.

Canto XVIII

We have all been swindled at one time or another, and nothing makes us angrier than to know that we have been swindled by someone that we trusted. Dante now devotes half of Hell to the description and punishment of the different ways that people swindle others.

Circle Eight, where Dante and Virgil find themselves after Geryon deposits them, is called the Malbowges. Shaped like a stone funnel, or an amphithe-

ater, as one critic describes it, it consists of ten
trenches dug into the rock with a stone path bridging
the trenches. In each trench, one of the kinds of simple fraud is punished.

NOTE: Fraud, for Dante, is the most offensive
sin, for it is the perversion for sinful purposes of the
one quality that separates man from other earthly
creatures—intellect. The sinner must think to plan his
deception. In Dante's malbowges, you will see how
fraud causes the disintegration of every kind of
human relationship, both personal and social. You
might pay special attention to the recurring image of a
city in corruption. When sexual favors, political
offices, religious offices, authority, money, and the
very language itself are fraudulent, the order and trust
that allows men to live and work together is gone.

   In the first of the trenches, bowge i, Dante sees two
streams of naked sinners running in opposite directions from one another, whipped by demons. These
are the Panderers and Seducers. Dante recognizes
Venedico Caccianemico, who supposedly sold his
own sister to another man's lust. He speaks to him
briefly but the demon's lash abruptly sends the sinner
prancing again with the rest. Virgil points out to Dante the shade of Jason who is punished for his seduc-
tions of Hysiphle and Medea in the Greek legends.
   The next image is perfect. Everyone has someone to
add to this crowd. Moving to the bridge that arches
over bowge ii, Dante hears whimpering and coughing
and the slapping of hands. Looking over, he sees the
foul trench of the Flatterers. The banks of this trench

are encrusted with scum; the fume rising to the bridge is horribly offensive. The trench is filled with Flatterers, who are wallowing in the actual excrement that they spewed metaphorically, in the form of words, on earth.

Dante looks for someone he might recognize and finds one whose head is thickly plastered with merd. When the sinner challenges Dante, asking why he stares more at him than at the others, Dante tells Allessio Intermini that he has seen him "dry-headed" on earth.

Virgil draws Dante's attention to another sinner, Thais, who alternately rises and crouches in the pool, each time repeating her famous line, a harlot's flattering lie. Our attention is probably drawn to her because she is more than a trafficker in flesh. She had defiled the language, as have all the inhabitants of this circle, defiling the possibility of communication between people.

NOTE: Dante's language is particularly vulgar in this canto and his descriptions are grotesque. Some translations refine the language more than others, but the level of coarseness is unmistakeable. You might be asked to leave class or the dinner table if you used it. So why does Dante use such graphic descriptions here and other places farther down in Hell?

As we said before, Dante uses language that matches his subject. The subject here is the depths of degradation possible to the sinner in his sin. Dante can't very well give a spiritual description, so he translates his concept into a physical description. Dante means no insult or lack of seriousness when he employs such low-style language. He simply means to communicate exactly what each sin is and what the consequences of choosing that sin are. You are what you do.

Canto XIX

Dante and Virgil continue on the path to bowge iii. Dante sees the trench filled with burning feet extending from holes in the ground. As Dante watches the kicking feet, he notices that one sinner thrashes particularly hard. When he asks Virgil about it, Virgil suggests that they go down into the bowge and let the sinner identify himself.

Dante speaks to the shade, Pope Nicholas III, who mistakenly thinks he is being addressed by Pope Boniface VIII. Dante corrects the misconception and lectures the Pope on the abuses of the Papacy, which makes the shade writhe and kick even harder. Virgil rewards Dante for this attack with an embrace and carries him out of the moat to the path. Apparently Dante is making some headway on his allegorical journey (at least until the next canto).

The inverted graves contain the Simoniacs, those who sold religious offices and favors. There is, apparently, one hole for all the Popes. As each who so abused the office dies, he forces the Popes who sinned in this way before him deeper into the hole and takes the place of his immediate predecessor.

NOTE: This is a strange punishment, but Dante gives us some help in trying to understand it. The image of the punishment is, again, the image of symbolic retribution. In a medieval baptismal font, the priest stands in a hole to pour water over the head of a person being welcomed to the Church. This is the first sacrament, that which opens the way to Heaven. Here is the inversion: the officer of the Church is embedded head first with feet aflame, welcomed to Hell for pursuing earthly power more than heavenly power.

Canto XX

Arriving at bowge iv, Dante sees sinners so twisted that they face the back of their bodies. Their eyes are filled with tears. These are the Sorcerers, the Fortune Tellers. Among them are Tiresias, the famous Greek prophet; Amphiaraus, one of the Seven against Thebes who foresaw his own death; and Manto, daughter of Tiresias. Seeing them, Dante weeps. Virgil chastises Dante severely for this sympathetic reaction, telling him that, "Here pity, or here piety, must die . . ." In other words, Dante, by showing pity at the results of God's judgment, is showing both an unreadiness to understand the true nature of sin and an arrogance at judging God's judgment. Dante pulls himself together as Virgil catalogs the sinners in this trench.

You are probably wondering why Dante is so moved by this particular punishment. We can only guess that Dante grieves over the twisted human forms. The Sorcerers themselves face backwards because they tried to see the future; their eyes are filled with tears so that those who tried to usurp God's power to penetrate the future can no longer even see in front of themselves. Dante's reaction and the rebuke from Virgil show that Dante's vision, too, is not clear enough for him to see beyond the immediate and the physical to the source and the reason beyond, the Divine Order of God.

Canto XXI

This and the next are probably the funniest cantos in the *Inferno*. They are like off-color satiric comedy. While you are reading, think whom you would like to reduce to such ridiculous stupidity.

Talking of various things, Virgil and Dante walk down the stone path until they come to bowge v, which is particularly dark. Looking into the bowge, Dante sees huge bubbles boiling up in a stream of sticky pitch. Virgil yells a warning and yanks Dante to a safer place to watch a huge demon approach, carrying a sinner over his shoulder. The demon hurls the sinner into the pitch, into the care of other demons who gleefully prod him with hooks while he stews. Virgil tells Dante to stay hidden behind a rock while he negotiates passage with the demons.

Virgil must curb the threatening demons with strong words before he is granted a conference with one appointed as spokesman. Virgil tries to intimidate the demon, who is not very cooperative, by letting him know this is a divine mission to show another person the depths and horrors of Hell. When the demon agrees to let them pass, Virgil calls Dante from his hiding place in the rocks. The demons tease and threaten Dante with pokes and prods. Dante cowers beside Virgil, who is hearing from the demons that the bridge on the path they are on is down and has been since the earthquake which followed the crucifixion of Christ. The spokesman does offer a demon-escort team to show the poets the way around part of the circle to another path.

Dante doesn't make any attempts to hide his fear and doubt, and is told by Virgil not to be afraid of the noise, which is meant for the sinners. The demons

line up to be dismissed by their spokesman-leader
and stick their tongues out at him in unison. He turns,
bends over, and sends them off with a fart that
sounds as loud as a bugle salute.

NOTE: The journey with the demons will continue in the next canto, but an explanation of the image
and the unusual tone is probably appropriate here.
Dante spends two entire cantos on this sin. He also
treats it with a tone of savage satire that is not evident
in other places in the *Inferno*, even as the sins grow
worse. Dante was banished from Florence for Barratry
or Graft, and so his particular interest in this sin is
understandable. (Barratry can mean either the sale of
public office or persistent hassling by law suits.)

Money sticks to the palms of Grafters, and so the
image of sticky pitch is appropriate. The demons are
probably parodies of various Florentine officials who
were responsible for Dante's exile. The grossness of
the demons, particularly the final salute, might be
part of Dante's revenge on those people who ruined
his life. (Don't the guardians look more ridiculous
than the sinners in this canto?)

Almost every critic felt it was necessary to say something about these cantos. Some call cantos XXI and
XXII the "Gargoyle cantos." Remember the comparison of the *Comedy* to a Gothic cathedral that we made
in the introduction? These two cantos would be the
grotesque corner gargoyles on the beautiful whole, if
we were to continue this metaphor. Other critics
explain the cantos in terms of Dante's intent to separate the blasphemous and profane in nether Hell II
from the merely obscene above. Despite the differences in opinion, it is interesting to note that so many
critics felt compelled to justify the existence of these
bawdy cantos within the intensely serious poem.

Canto XXII

Dante and Virgil set off with their escort of demons. Dante sees the sinners surface slightly in the river of pitch, and then hide at the sight of the demons who try to fork them out. One of the Barrators does not duck fast enough and is hooked by one of the demons. The demons torment him for a while. Hoping to gain his freedom, the sinner offers to lure others from the moat to where the demons will have more luck finding them. The demons agree, but the sinner takes advantage of their momentary lapse of attention to dive back into the pitch and escape. Two of the demons, furious at being duped, begin to fight each other so viciously that they both end up in the pitch. The poets, fearing the unpredictable wrath of the demons, leave quickly and continue on their way.

You can see here that, as orderly and contained as Hell might appear, there is no justice, order, or discipline in Hell's ranks. When the guards themselves turn on each other with savagery, you see all at once the nature of this place, the untrustworthiness of the fraudulent, and Dante's feelings about the lack of integrity and dignity of the Florentine officials who banished him. You will also see here, as well as farther down in Hell, why Dante is often called the "master of the disgusting."

Canto XXIII

The poets do well to fear that they will be chased by the demons so bent on anger. Dante barely has mentioned this apprehension when they see two demons coming after them. Virgil scoops Dante up like a baby to his breast, and they flee down the upper bank of bowge vi. When Virgil sets Dante down on the bottom of this circle, Dante can see the pursuing demons on the cliffs overhead.

When Dante finally feels safe enough to turn his attention to this new bowge, he sees sinners decked with paint and walking in slow, slow steps. Each of these sinners, the Hypocrites, wears a long hooded cloak that hides his identity. The cloaks hide the sinners just as they sought to hide their true intentions or feelings beneath a bright facade on earth. Dante begs Virgil to look for a recognizeable sinner so he can question him about the robes. Hearing the voice, a shade far in back of the crowd tells Dante to slow down so he can catch up and speak to him. Dante waits and is approached by two Jovial Friars, Catalano and Loderingo, who explain that the cloaks are lined with lead so heavy that they are very difficult to carry and balance.

The conversation is cut short when Dante sees one shade crucified on the ground with three stakes forced through him. The Friars explain that this is Caiaphas, the high priest of the Jews, who counseled the Pharisees that Jesus should be sacrificed as a public expediency. For this, he is crucified where all the Hypocrites with their leaden cloaks must walk over him, thus forcing him, as chief hypocrite, to bear the weight of the hypocrisy of the world.

Dante and Virgil find they have been given bad directions by the demons. The Friars tell them that the bridge is down but that they could scale the rocks to the spur ahead, and from there continue with the journey. Virgil leaves in a huff; Dante follows.

Canto XXIV

The path the Friars indicated is far more difficult than Dante imagined. He and Virgil must scale the rocky wall, measuring each move and heaving their

weight to the next foothold. Virgil does most of the
hoisting and Dante does most of the panting, so when
the poets do reach the top and Dante sits down to
rest, Virgil criticizes his laziness. Dante, ashamed,
tells Virgil that he is resolute. They climb the steep
arch of the seventh bridge, again no small task, and
Dante hears voices from the trench below. He asks
Virgil if they can cross over this bridge and climb
down the far wall into bowge vii to inspect what they
can't see from above in the darkness. As he does
whenever Dante makes any move to understand
actively what he is experiencing, Virgil readily
agrees.

The trench is like something from a nightmare. It is
filled with a mass of serpents and reptiles, swarming
and repulsive. Over this mass run naked men, whose
hands are tied behind with snakes that curl and loop
through the loins of the men. Dante sees a shade run
by; a snake darts up and stings the sinner on the neck.
Immediately the sinner bursts into flames, burns, and
crumbles to ash. Just as rapidly, the forms grow again
out of the ashes, stunned and bewildered with the
pain.

Virgil approaches the sinner and asks who he is and
what he has done to deserve such a fate. Vanni Fucci
identifies himself as a Thief cast here because he stole
the treasury of the sacristy. (History tells of additional
sides to Vanni Fucci. He escaped, allowing an inno-
cent man to be jailed for a year for the crime he had
committed before Fucci's accomplices were hanged.)
Vanni Fucci tells Dante that his worst shame is having
Dante find him here and goes on to give Dante a
threatening prophecy of events in Florence, with
hope that the news hurts Dante.

Canto XXV

Vanni Fucci, in his rage, gives "the figs," an obscene gesture, to God, is immediately aswarm with serpents, and flees. Cacus, a centaur, also encircled with snakes and carrying a fire-breathing dragon on his back, chases the wretched Thief.

The next scene would be a real challenge to a movie maker or a special-effects artist. The imagination it displays is astounding. As the attention of the poet is drawn to the arrival of three sinners, Dante feels he has to beg the reader to believe the description of the next series of events.

A six-legged worm leaps, catches one of the Thieves with all of his legs, and takes the sinner's face in his mouth. Dante watches in awe as the two forms melt into one perverse form, so wretched that it defies description. The melded monstrosity moves slowly out of sight as a lizard scampers into view. It faces one of the sinners, leaps, and takes a huge bite out of the sinner's throat. From both the wound and the lizard's mouth smoke emerges and the streams of smoke blend. As they do, the two forms begin a very strange metamorphosis, each shriveling or sprouting where necessary to deform and reform as the other, the man becoming the lizard and the lizard the man. Dante swears that, although he was bewildered by the scene, the description is accurate.

NOTE: Because the main tool of the thief is his hands, the hands of the Thieves are bound. Because the Thieves made no distinction between what's yours and what's mine, they are deprived of any distinct form. Because stealing has such reptilian sneakiness, the Thieves continually exchange shapes with reptiles, and then attack other Thieves to rid themselves of their reptilian forms. The punishment is certainly understandable for those who chose to ignore the ownership of goods, which, in Dante's age, were considered extensions of the owner himself.

Canto XXVI

Dante takes a satiric swipe at Florence before getting back to the story of his journey. He says that he has seen five of that city's members in the ring of the Thieves. He also suggests that more evil will come to Florence as a result of her sins.

The poets climb up the rocky spur to the next bridge, which arches over bowge viii, containing the souls of the Counselors of Fraud. Dante describes what looks to him like a mass of fireflies. As he gets closer, he peers intently and gathers that each flame walking on the bottom of the bowge contains a sinner. Seeing him study the scene with such fervor, Virgil affirms what Dante has already guessed. For Dante's quest, this is a good sign. He is beginning to see for himself what has needed explanation before.

Dante does ask Virgil to identify two shades who occupy the same flame. Virgil explains that they are Ulysses and Diomede. At once Dante asks if he might speak with them. He tells Virgil that he is aware that he cannot approach them himself and implores Virgil to intercede.

NOTE: We'll have to remember a little classical legend to understand this exchange. Ulysses (you may know him as Odysseus) and Diomede were Greeks who fought against Troy in the Trojan War. Ulysses was the creator of the Trojan Horse, the deciding factor against the Trojans. Aeneas, the hero of Virgil's epic, was a surviving Trojan who fled the sacking of Troy and set off to found a new Troy, namely Rome; Virgil, being a Roman, would therefore be a descendant of the enemy, and Dante, an Italian, was also a distant descendant of the defeated Trojans.

Dante knows if he speaks to the Greeks in Italian, they will ignore him. Virgil, however, being the White Magician, and aided here by divine assistance, can compel the spirits to speak.

When the twin sepulchered spirits approach, Virgil uses the formula for conjuration to make the two spirits stop and tell their story. It is interesting that the spirits do not speak to the poets. Rather, Ulysses tells his story as though he has been programmed and has told it many times before. Several explanations have been offered for this. Perhaps because Ulysses' sin has been the abuse of the power of the tongue, the shade can no longer have control over his speech. Nevertheless, Ulysses' speech is moving. True, he deceived his men by convincing them to sail to the ends of the earth with him, but he cannot disguise the glorious hunger for adventure that motivated him. Even this low in Hell, Dante allows his own sympathy to surface, though he accepts God's judgment.

The Counselors of Fraud have abused the gifts they have been given by God, particularly the gifts of genius and speech. Dante should have lived to see our advertising or our political conventions. (Dante himself says in this canto that he, a poet, must take special care not to abuse the same gifts.) Because these sinners have deceived other men and hidden their motives, they are hidden. The flame serves two purposes: one, to suggest the destruction that the sinners have caused and, two, to parody in the tongues of flame the gift of tongues that has been defiled.

Canto XXVII

When the Greek spirit finishes his recitation, Virgil dismisses the shades. Another tall flame approaches making a strange sound. As the sounds are transmitted up the flame, they become intelligible to the poets. This flame contains the soul of Guido da Montefeltro of Romagna. Dante gives him a summary of recent happenings, none of which is good news to the shade. It is again noticeable here that, although all the shades seem to be able to foresee the future and are aware of things in the distant past, the present and the recent past are denied them. This might be one of the ways that Dante creates an "eternal present" as his concept of eternity. After the shade has heard the news, he tells Dante his own story.

NOTE: Guido was an influential and intelligent Ghibelline soldier who had resigned to become a Franciscan monk and save his soul. At the Pope's insistence, he got involved in a dispute between the reigning Pope, Boniface VIII, and another powerful family who had retreated to a large castle. Guido negotiated and pursuaded the family to leave the castle to accept a fair treaty being offered by the Pope. They did. The Pope promptly destroyed the castle.

It seems unfair that Guido should suffer, and he does tell Dante that St. Francis came to rescue his soul when he died, but St. Francis was stopped by one of the Black Angels. Though the Pope had absolved Guido beforehand, Guido never repented after his deed. The Black Angel tells St. Francis that absolution is not

valid when the sinner is intending to commit the sin.
And so Minos gave Guido eight coils of his tail and
here he is.

Canto XXVIII

How much worse can Hell get? Dante begins the
next canto with a direct address to you, the reader. He
says the next sight, bowge ix, which houses the Sowers of Discord, is so awful that he is not sure any
words will describe it. He claims if all the wounded in
a long list of battles were to display their wounds and
pieces and blood, the sight would not be as horrible as
the one he meets here.

The sinners are continually cut apart by a demon
with a bloody sword. After each wounding, the sinner must travel around the circle, dragging his own
severed part. As the sinner proceeds, the parts heal
and he returns full circle, only to be hacked apart
again. The severing sword is a fairly obvious symbolic
retribution for those who have used their intellect to
separate those meant to be united. Each suffers
according to the severity of the sin.

Dante sees one sinner cut down the middle. Don't
read this section before eating, because Dante spares
none of the details or the coarse language as he
describes the exposed digestive tract and all its now-
dangling parts. This is Muhammad (or Mahomet), the
leader of the schism between Christianity and Islam.
In front of him is his son-in-law, Ali, whose head is
split open. These are Sowers of Religious Discord. It is
not hard to guess Dante's opinion of this religious
group from the description he offers. (Obviously not
very ecumenical, Dante wrote from strict Catholic
doctrine.) Muhammad tells Dante the particulars of
this punishment and offers a warning to Fra Dolcino,

a supposed schismatic still alive on earth.

Dante sees another mutilated sinner. On this one, the nose has been cut off, the ear lopped off, and the gullet pierced. This is Pier da Medicina, and his wounds indicate his intrigues in Romagna: the ear of the eavesdropper, the nose of the snoop, and the throat of the liar. Pier is one of the Sowers of Civil Discord. He speaks to Dante and asks him to take the message of what he has seen to earth. While speaking, he shows Dante the now-mute Curio, tongue hacked from his head for advising Julius Caesar to cross the Rubicon. Mosca dei Lamberti, severed hands held up and covering his face with bloody clots, enters the conversation. Dante greets him with a wish for a death to all of Mosca's family. (If you think Dante is cruel to this sinner, wait a few cantos.)

Dante the author intercedes once again to warn you that the next description sounds so unbelievable that he might be tempted to doubt his own judgment, if he were not under such powerful care. He claims that he can still see the sinner running toward him, swinging his head in his hand like a lantern. When the sinner, Bertrand de Born, reaches the bridge, he tosses his head up in the air so it can talk to Dante, who is standing on the bridge. Bertrand tells Dante his head has been severed because he counseled a son to overthrow his father.

NOTE: What would Dante have thought of the blood-and-guts in our movies and television shows? Dante is graphically violent, but for the purpose of showing how repulsive man can become. Can we so clearly justify the extent of the violence in our entertainment?

Canto XXIX

Dante lingers on the edge of bowge ix, looking for one of his relatives, Geri del Bello. Virgil tells Dante to leave him to his punishment and to put his mind on higher matters. As they walk, Virgil tells Dante that, while Dante was talking to the other Sowers of Discord, Geri del Bello passed and made threatening gestures toward Dante.

The poets come to the last bowge where the Falsifiers are stricken with diseases and afflictions of all the senses. The noise causes Dante to cover his ears. Some are lying, hardly able to move. Two are propped against each other, back to back, each viciously scratching himself, peeling off flakes of himself like scales from a fish. When Dante speaks to them, they identify themselves as Griffilino D'Arezzo and Capocchio. Although each was also guilty of other sins on earth, they are placed here because this is the circle were the most offensive of their sins, alchemy, is punished.

These sinners falsified goods. For that, all their senses and their bodies are made impure, made sick. Other kinds of Falsifiers will be mentioned in the next canto, but you should notice that this is the last sin of the Malbowges. The Malbowges began with the Panderers and Seducers, those who sold the sexual relationship, and ends with those who deceive others in the products they produce. Think of how you feel when you pay good money for a book or a record, only to find it's a cheap rip-off. Wouldn't you like to see the people responsible get kicked down to bowge x?

NOTE: Looking at this circle, we can see a degeneration of the spirit, which now recognizes no obligation to be honest in any of its relationships with other men. All the means of communication—speech, Church, State, even money itself—are corrupted. Dante makes clear the state of the spirit by continuing the image of the city, now in its terminal stages of disease.

Canto XXX

Just as Capocchio finishes telling Dante his story, two horrible spirits come racing through the bowge and grab Capocchio. One sinks his teeth into Capocchio's neck and they drag him away. Griffilino explains that these shades are Myrrha and Gianni Schicchi.

NOTE: Myrrha was a woman who disguised herself and slipped into her father's bed. When he discovered the trick, he threatened to kill her. Instead, she fled and turned herself into a myrtle tree, from which Adonis was later born. Gianni Schicchi pretended to be a recently dead man in order to dictate a new will for that man, which would be favorable to a friend and himself. These sinners are the Imposters, the Falsifiers of Person.

When the pair of sinners departs, Dante sees another sinner who lies distorted, bloated, and parched. The sinner asks Dante why he walks free of punishment. This is Master Adam who reportedly counterfeited so many gold coins that he jeopardized the currency of Tuscany. For this he was burned; here he continues to burn with an eternal thirst that prevents him from thinking of anything else, except the revenge he would impart on his fellow sinners.

Dante asks Master Adam about another pair of sinners who appear to be rolled together and strangely immobile. Master Adam tells Dante that they haven't moved since he arrived and identifies one as Sinon of Troy, the Greek spy who persuaded the Trojans to open the gates to the Trojan Horse. Just then, Sinon rises and belts Master Adam so hard on the belly that it sounds like a drum. Master Adam responds with an arm square across the face of Sinon. The two argue back and forth so furiously that Dante becomes grossly intent on the argument. Virgil rebukes Dante, telling him that if he keeps watching, he will risk an argument with Virgil. Dante is terribly ashamed, speechless. Virgil gently accepts Dante's unspoken apology, telling Dante that to enjoy such a sight is vulgar.

Although Dante's quest is to order his experience and to understand why each sin is punished the way it is and where it is, enjoying the punishment is not part of the job. Dante has to learn to be repulsed by sin and to understand that each sight he sees is the image of a soul so frozen in sin that he has forgone change, Heaven, and God. Virgil rebukes Dante for concentrating on the grotesqueness of the individual and not seeing him in terms of the essential rightness of God's Divine Order.

Canto XXXI

Virgil and Dante climb the path in semidarkness and head toward the pit that houses Satan. In the darkness, Dante thinks he sees a series of towers and asks Virgil what city they are approaching. Virgil tells Dante he will see more clearly as they get closer; then he decides it is best to tell Dante about what he is to see before he becomes too frightened. When they reach the wall of the well, he tells Dante he will see the

Giants and the Titans who fought the gods, frozen to their navels in the ice.

Despite Virgil's warnings, Dante becomes more and more frightened as the sight becomes clearer. Nevertheless, Dante has the presence of mind to think that it was wise that Nature stopped making Giants, for a thinking mind joined to such strength and malice would be too much for a man to defend himself against.

One of the huge monsters begins to howl in a language Dante does not understand. Virgil explains that this Giant is Nimrod, who was responsible, according to the myths, for the Tower of Babel.

The poets continue to walk and come upon another Giant who is not only frozen in the earth but has a chain wound around him five times, binding the left hand in front of him and the right hand in back. (The left hand symbolizes evil, while the right hand is supposed to be good.) When Dante learns from Virgil that this is Ephialtes, who was killed by Apollo in the battle against the gods, Dante asks if they might not see Briareus, his famous fellow-fighter with fifty heads and one hundred arms. Virgil tells Dante that Briareus is too far away, yet describes him as twice as fierce as Ephialtes and bound in the same way. Instead, the poets seek Antaeus, who is not bound to the earth because he did not fight the gods.

At this point, Ephialtes begins to thrash about so hard that Dante says he would have feared for his life had he not remembered the Giant was chained. The poets find Antaeus, who responds to Virgil's flattery and the promise that Dante will make him famous on earth. He gently lifts the poets and places them down on the surface of the frozen lake, Cocytus, the bottom of the pit of Hell.

NOTE: You may ask why Dante has the Giants guarding this, the very bottom of Hell. It's a good question. Possibly they represent the possibility of power without the controlling influence of love and reason. The Giants are very proud. Notice Antaeus' response to Virgil's flattery. Most of them revolted against the gods and thus share or represent Satan's place as the one who revolted against God. Unloosed, these Giants would reduce to uncontrollable chaos the order that God has created. As representatives of the basic earth-primitive forces in the human spirit, we see that Dante feels they must be contained, or else the world would be run by the forces of stupidity, vanity, violence, and treachery.

Canto XXXII

Just as you are wondering what could possibly be at the bottom of Hell, Dante now apologizes in advance for any inability to describe what he sees. It's small wonder that he has doubts. This is the Ninth Circle, where the most loathesome of the sinners, Traitors, are frozen into Cocytus. Two images, that of the lake and that of freezing, work to create Dante's final picture of the soul who has turned ultimately from God.

The lake is the collection of all the sin, refuse, and defilement that descends from earth, from Hell, and from the river Lethe, which runs through Purgatory and washes the purged sins back to Cocytus. It is, therefore, the center or the core of sin. The ice clearly portrays the painful numbness of the sinners and the immobility of their souls, now locked in by cruelty and treachery. Together, these images present the inversion and perversion of the qualities of the Celestial City in this place in the universe farthest from God.

As Dante is turning around to look, Virgil warns him not to trample the heads of the sinners. The heads of the sinners, bowed, teeth uncontrollably chattering, discolored from the cold, protrude from the ice. This first region in Cocytus is Caina, named for Cain, who in the Bible, slew his brother over an inheritance. Here the Traitors against Kin are frozen with enough freedom to allow their heads to bow and tears to run unobstructed. (If you are thinking this is unimportant, remember the last time you got a pain behind your eye from eating ice cream too fast. Do you want to spend an eternity like that?)

Dante takes in the whole vision and returns to the sight at his feet, two souls frozen breast to breast so that, it seems to Dante, their hair has grown together. Dante speaks to the two and they raise their heads to answer. As a consequence, the cold freezes their tears and locks their heads together. In fury, the two sinners butt their heads against each other and rock madly. Another sinner, who is frozen nearby and has lost two ears to frostbite, asks Dante why he is looking so hard at the pair. He goes on to identify them as Napoleone and Allessandro degli Alberti, brothers who killed each other in a quarrel over politics and their inheritance. The reporting sinner also draws Dante's attention to other inhabitants of Caina, Focaccia and Sassol Mascheroni, before identifying himself as Camiscion de' Pazzi whose sins, he says, will seem less cruel when seen beside those committed by other members of his family. (Camiscion murdered a kinsman who was a traitor to his country, a White Guelph who surrendered for a bribe a castle he was supposed to defend.)

Walking and thinking about the unforgettable sight, Dante inadvertently kicks one of the Traitors in the face and gets a shrill rebuke. Dante begs Virgil, who is hurrying ahead, to wait just a moment. He has a hunch he knows this sinner. Dante asks the still-cursing sinner who he is. The sinner responds by asking who Dante thinks he is, to go through kicking people in the face. Dante again tries to get the sinner to identify himself by promising him fame on earth. The sinner replies that he wants just the opposite and that Dante shows a lack of wit when he tries that approach in this region of Hell. (This region is Antenora, named for Antenor, who supposedly betrayed Troy to the Greeks. Traitors against their Country are cast here.)

Readers who remember the compassionate Dante who fainted at the story of Francesca and Paolo in the First Circle of Hell are shocked at the response Dante now gives this sinner. Dante grabs him by the hair and threatens to pull it out, tuft by tuft, if he doesn't identify himself. Again, the sinner refuses even to look at Dante, telling him that he can strip his head a thousand fruitless times. Enraged, Dante yanks a handful of hair from the scalp. The shade yelps, which provokes another sinner, Buoso da Duera, to chastise him for barking out and disturbing everyone; he calls out the sinner's name, Bocca degli Abati. Dante, hearing Bocca's name, calls him a filthy traitor and assures him that his name will be known. Responding, Bocca tells Dante not to forget the story of the chatterbox who informed on him.

The sinners like to tell on each other, but are very reluctant to identify themselves. Thus, they continue the cruel and selfish treachery that landed them there.

NOTE: Is Dante too cruel to Bocca? You will have to decide that for yourself. The Traitors are cruel; maybe they should be treated cruelly. Dante's cruelty, on the allegorical level, looks like a successful reaction to a terrible sin. Can we see Dante's anger as part of the repulsion he feels at sin? When you see someone who has done something cruel and deceitful to another person, aren't you angry at him even though he didn't do a thing to you?

Dante leaves Bocca and comes upon one of the most horrible sights in Hell, two sinners frozen together, one gnawing the skull and brain of the other. Dante begs the sinner to tell him who he is and why he is condemned to this hateful display of rage.

Canto XXXIII

What is more repulsive than cannibalism? Picture this final scene of human depravity. Dante speaks to the two sinners in the filthy ice. One lifts his head from his feast, wipes the blood and brains from his chin on the remaining hair of the skull he has been chewing, and then answers. What could these sinners have done that is so disgusting as to deserve this punishment?

The two are Roger (Ruggieri degli Abaldini) and Ugolino (Count Ugolino della Gherardesca) who were involved in a plot and counterplot to seize power.

Ugolino and his grandson, Nino, were rival heads of families. In order to get rid of Nino, Ugolino allied himself with Archbishop Roger. Once Nino was out of power, Roger turned on Ugolino. Ugolino, his two sons, and two of his grandsons were imprisoned in a tower for months. After this long imprisonment, Ugolino woke one morning to the sound of the tower doors being nailed shut. The family was left to starve.

Dante knows how to throw in an emotional clincher to sway a jury! Ugolino tells Dante that when he bit his hand to stop from crying, one of the boys mistook the gesture as one of hunger and offered up his own flesh to Ugolino. Horrible as Ugolino's fate is, we must wish an even worse fate on Roger, who caused Ugolino's tragedy. Ugolino renews his savage chewing.

NOTE: Roger and Ugolino are the last of the pairs of sinners. If you think back, you'll remember several notable pairs: Paolo and Francesca, Ulysses and Diomede, Farinata and Cavalcante. Why does Dante use them? Are there any special ties here?

First comparison works. You can say a lot about a person simply by placing him, literally or figuratively, next to another. (Think of how many similes and metaphors you have had to identify over the years.) The lines that introduce the stories of Paolo and Francesca and of Roger and Ugolino are drawn from the same passage of Virgil. As we have been noticing all along, Dante seems to have left nothing to chance, so this is probably not an accident. The lovers are in the First Circle; the traitors are in the last.

Reinforcing the comparison, Dante emphasizes this final image of mutual sin. Remember how Francesca wept as she told her story, took the blame for the mutual sin, and, even in Hell, saw beauty in Paolo? Although they had sinned, there is still love and trust. Looking at Roger and Ugolino—the starver serving as food for cannibalism, the hatred that seems to grow with each mouthful—we see the end of any possible human relationship. This truly is Dante's image of sin as a devouring passion for destruction.

The final sinners whom Dante encounters in his journey through Hell are the Treacherous against Guests and Host. They are frozen face up in the ice of the last ring of Cocytus, which is Ptolemea, named for Ptolomeus, who slaughtered his father-in-law at a banquet. You are probably wondering why this is the most serious wrong. After all, you see horrible kidnappings and murders in the papers all the time. What makes this sin so wrong? Some of you may even remember this sin as a major issue in *Macbeth* and in the history of the House of Atreus in the Aeschylus trilogy, the *Oresteia*.

For the only explanation we can offer, look back at Dante's concept of the universe, especially at the idea of hierarchy. Stability and order are based on each person and each thing staying in his proper place and doing well with his particular responsibilities. To threaten or plot against the leaders of any society is a capital crime because it threatens the order and security of the entire group. In Dante's time, with society structured in a far more hierarchical, far less democratic way, the sin must have seemed even worse.

Here Dante speaks to Friar Albergio, who deceived and slaughtered his brother. Dante promises, in return for the man's story, to undo the ice which forms from the pools of tears the prone sinner weeps, forcing the sinner to weep inwardly. After hearing the friar's story, and seeing Branca d'Oria pointed out,

Dante refuses to remove the ice and calls such churlishness "a courtesy."

NOTE: Two things bother students immensely here. One, Branca d'Oria is still alive, yet his soul is in Hell. This doesn't seem to fit with Dante's whole concept of free will as the source of eternal placement. Couldn't the man repent, start making amends, and be sent to Purgatory? If we remember that this poem is at least partly allegory, we might be able to explain this as an image of the soul in the depths of sin. It is so frozen away from God and into the will to sin that it probably can't find its way even to begin repentance. In other words, Dante might be trying to suggest a condition of the spirit rather than an actual happening or point of doctrine.

The other thing that students find hard to buy is Dante's refusal to remove the ice from the Friar's eyes after he promises to do so. Is this simple cruelty? It looks as though Dante is doing exactly what the sinners are being punished for—being insincere and untrustworthy. Before we judge, let's raise a question. Can you be kind and fair to everyone on earth? Would or could you be fair to a Hitler? Fairness is based on mutual trust; sinners this treacherous can't be trusted. In this place of treachery, there is no place for honesty. Even Virgil had to flatter the Giants to get here. Also, if we remember that part of Dante's journey is the moral and allegorical journey to understand exactly what sin is, we can see his cruelty as progress. Dante now sees sin for the perversion that it is and is learning to guard himself against it.

Canto XXXIV

How do you picture Satan? Is he an active tempter as in Milton's *Paradise Lost*, Goethe's *Faust*, or Marlowe's *Dr. Faustus?* Here Satan appears as the end of Dante's image of sin frozen in the wastes of the world.

Dante looks up from the ice that holds completely submerged sinners (this is Judecca, home of the Traitors against God and Leader, named after the Bible's Judas) to see a huge, shadowy form. A blast of wind is so severe that Dante has to hide behind Virgil to escape it. When Dante looks again, he sees what he won't even try to explain: Satan.

Satan is huge. Some critics who have calculated the mathematical clues in the *Inferno* measure him somewhere between 1000 and 1500 feet long. Satan is frozen to his chest in the ice but his three sets of wings are free to beat. Ironically, Satan beats these wings in a furious eternal attempt to escape, but it is these wings that keep him frozen in the one place in the universe farthest from God. Satan has three faces (red, yellow, and black) and each chews on a sinner. The sinner in the middle, head first in Satan's mouth, is continually stripped of his flesh by Satan's clawing hands. This is Judas, the apostle who betrayed Christ and set in motion the crucifixion. In the other two mouths are Julius Caesar's assassins, Brutus and Cassius.

NOTE: Readers of Shakespeare's *Julius Caesar* are probably protesting heavily at this point. Our interpretation of Cassius and Brutus is colored heavily by the play and our own democratic principles. Dante probably had no special affection for Julius Caesar as a person, but looked at him as the founder of the Roman Empire which, in Dante's eyes, made possible the spread of Christianity. Cassius and Brutus are punished like this for treason against the Roman Empire and for breaking a sworn oath of allegiance to Caesar.

Satan himself is the image of a perverse or an inverted Trinity. The Trinity has three separate beings, Father, Son, and Holy Spirit, which are united in one being (the major mystery of the Trinity); Satan is one being divided into three—three faces, three sets of wings, three colors, etc. Whereas the power of the Trinity can elevate and draw all things toward Itself, Satan's futile beatings only freeze him more solidly where he is. Satan is frozen into the scum of the universe (see Canto XXXII for the description) while God is the source of all light, warmth, love, and so on.

After Dante takes this all in, Virgil reminds Dante that they still have to get past Satan. This could be a problem. They time their move and, while the wings are unfurled and lifted, rush in, grab the fur of Satan, and begin the descent. At least Virgil does; Dante is clinging to his back. At the hip joint, Virgil turns and starts to climb up. Panting with the effort, Virgil reaches a place where the rock forms a small ledge. He puts Dante on the ledge and crawls out himself. Dante looks up, expecting to see Satan's head and Hell, but sees instead his legs and, at a distance, the morning sky.

You science majors should have this all figured out. Dante needs Virgil to explain how they seemed to turn around, but didn't, and how they could leave Hell in the evening, travel no more than half an hour, and arrive in the morning. The answer is that they have passed the center of gravity. Virgil had to turn and climb up the legs because Satan's hip joint was at that center of gravity. As regards the time, Virgil explains that the morning sun Dante sees is the sun of the southern hemisphere, which is twelve hours behind the sun of the northern hemisphere they have left on the other side of Hell. It is now Holy Saturday morning again.

Virgil gives Dante one more instruction: "Up on thy legs." The two start to follow a small stream, the Lethe, which drains from Mount Purgatory, where they are headed. Although your journey through the *Inferno* is completed, Dante has Purgatory and Heaven yet to travel.

A STEP BEYOND

Tests and Answers

TESTS

Test 1

1. The rings of Hell in Dante's vision _____
   A. are arranged in the order in which the sins were committed in time.
   B. contain sinners arranged in the chronological order of their lives.
   C. are arranged in degrees of evil of the sin, the most sinful closest to the center of the earth.
   D. contain only the contemporaries of Dante.

2. Which of the following descriptions of Satan is _____ accurate?
   A. He has three sets of wings that he beats continuously.
   B. He has three faces and each of the faces is chewing a traitor.
   C. He is frozen in the bottom of Hell.
   D. All of the above are correct.

3. Dante's journey through Hell can be seen as _____ symbolic of the thematic statement that
   A. certain souls are chosen to fight the battle of good against evil.
   B. understanding the nature of sin is possible only to those of extraordinary intellect.
   C. salvation is attainable to those willing to commit themselves to an active pursuit of it.

    D. man often goes through long, unnecessary journeys to reach his ultimate goals.

4. Why does Dante place Satan in the middle of earth?   _____

    A. There are enough monsters there to prevent him from escaping.

    B. From that point, he is equidistant from all the points on earth and has equal access to the souls from all nations.

    C. Satan gathers his power and energy from the energy at the center of gravity.

    D. According to the Ptolemaic world view, it is the point farthest from God.

5. Dante finds himself, at the beginning of the *Inferno*, lost in the Dark Wood. What explanation does he offer for being there?   _____

    A. He was led there by Beatrice and the three animals.

    B. He has not been sufficiently active in the pursuit of God.

    C. He was led there by Virgil.

    D. He offers no explanation for this placement.

6. Briefly explain why Dante ordered the sins he included in Hell the way he did.

7. Select a famous person who was born after 1321 (the year of Dante's death) whom you are fairly certain Dante might have included had he known him or her. Tell where in the *Inferno* you think Dante would have placed this person and why.

8. Explain why Virgil was chosen as Dante's guide.

9. "Dante's language and style reflect the reality he is describing." Support this statement with direct references to one specific canto.

10. Compare and contrast two pairs of sinners in the *Inferno* and explain why they are used.

Test 2

1. One of the themes of the *Inferno* is related to _____
Virgil's continual chastisement of Dante's fail-
ure to question. Which of the following best
expresses this theme? Attainment of Heaven
   A. can only be reached after sufficient pun-
      ishment at the hands of someone denied
      Heaven.
   B. can only be reached through an under-
      standing of the nature of God and the
      structure of his universe.
   C. can be reached only after an extended peri-
      od of doubt as to its existence.
   D. is reserved for those who rely on reason
      rather than faith.

2. In certain cantos of the *Inferno*, Dante's style is _____
coarse and uncomfortable. In others, it is
smooth and flowing. Which of the following
statements best explains this?
   A. Dante was unsure about the truth or accu-
      racy of his vision of the universe. The style
      changes reflect periods of doubt in Dante's
      faith.
   B. Dante had two visions of the universe, one
      from the Catholic Church and one that
      was his own personal vision. The conflict
      in style represents the conflict in images.
   C. Dante felt the occasional use of an uncom-
      fortable style would encourage a reader to
      move through his long and complex
      work.

    D. For Dante, style changes with the subject.
When he was describing the grotesque
nature of sin, the style was harsh. When
he was describing the grandeur of the universe, the style matched the subject.

3. At the beginning of the *Inferno*, Dante finds   _____
himself lost in the Dark Wood and
    A. besieged by the Furies who are threaten-
ing to call Medusa.
    B. challenged by a lion, a leopard, and a she-
wolf.
    C. having visions of Beatrice, St. Lucy, and
the Virgin.
    D. frightened by the Fallen Angels who
guard the gate to Hell.

Read the following excerpt from Canto XX (Sorcerers) and
use it to answer questions 4 and 5.

> And, Reader, so God give thee grace to glean
> Profit of my book, think if I could be left
> Dry-eyed, when close before me I had seen
>
> Our image so distorted, so bereft
> Of dignity, that their eyes' brimming pools
> Spilled down to bathe the buttocks at the cleft.
>
> Truly I wept, leaned on the pinnacles
> Of the hard rock; until my guide said, "Why!
> And art thou too like all the other fools?
>
> Here pity, or here piety, must die
> If the other lives; who's wickeder than one
> That's agonized by God's high equity?"

4. Dante is agonizing over the twisted bodies of   _____
the sorcerers. Why is Virgil chastising him?
    A. Dante is failing in his quest to move from
the perception of Hell's horrors to understanding the nature of sin.

B. Dante's emoting is taking up too much time, and Virgil is threatening to leave him there to weep.

C. Virgil knows that one must remain completely emotionless if one wants to make it through Hell.

D. Virgil is impatient with Dante's "On again-off again" sympathy toward the souls in Hell and wants him to be consistently sympathetic.

5. In this passage, Virgil expresses a concept of Hell and the sinners in Hell which Dante does not yet have. Which statement below best expresses *Virgil's* concept of the sinners in Hell? _____

A. Although the placement in Hell is haphazard and there is no order in Hell, the placement is eternal and must therefore be *accepted*.

B. Each place in Hell was chosen by the *victim* of the sinner, and is therefore ultimately just.

C. Sinners *choose* Hell by choosing sin, and the placement in Hell is arranged, as is everything, by the greater wisdom and order of God.

D. Hell is a place of *purification*, and each soul, although now suffering, will ultimately be released to join God.

6. Select one sin and its punishment. Use it to demonstrate that Dante's Hell is one of symbolic retribution.

7. How is the *Inferno* an allegory?

8. Suppose at the end of the journey through Hell, when Virgil tells Dante, "Up on your feet," Dante responds something like this: "Look! What do you want from me? I'm only human. I will not walk another step." What would this mean in terms of Dante's quest and in terms of the meaning of the work?

9. Knowing from Cantos XIII–XV how Dante feels about maintaining natural elements, explain how you think he would react to such things as diet pills, steroids, and birth-control pills.

10. In Dante's *Inferno* you will find his contemporaries, people from the past, and various mythological and legendary beings. Explain why.

ANSWERS

Test 1

1. C   2. D   3. C   4. D   5. B

6. Dante arranged his sins according to the severity of the sins. Sin, for Dante, is a freezing of the will away from God and grace. The more the sin involved a choice, an appetite, or intellectual planning, the worse it was, and the farther from God it was placed.

   The description of Hell (in the Setting section of this guide) and of Dante's quest (in The Characters section) will give more detailed explanations. The transitions from one type of sin to another (Cantos VIII, IX, and XVIII) also offer some explanations.

7. The answers to this question will obviously depend on the person selected. If the person is guilty of more than one kind of sin, he would be placed in the circle of his worst sin. Hitler, for example, was guilty of massive violence but would be punished far below Phlegethon.

Whether he would be a Sower of Discord or a Traitor would depend on how you interpret his intentions in Germany.

8. Both historically and figuratively, Virgil makes sense as a guide. He serves on several of the levels that we have discussed. For a full review of Virgil's importance to the *Inferno*, see the section on Virgil in The Characters section of this guide. See also the justification of Virgil's "nagging" in the discussion of Canto IV.

9. Several cantos will work especially well for this question: III, XVIII, XXI, XXII, XXVIII, and XXXIII. In each of these, Dante is describing vile sins and their image in the physical condition of the sinner. Dante means no insult or lack of seriousness when he uses gross images and obscene predicaments. He feels that the physical and spiritual worlds are closely related and uses the sensual images from the physical world to describe what can't be sensed in the spiritual world.

10. A pair of pairs that could be used is Francesca-Paolo and Roger-Ugolino. A discussion of some of the ways Dante suggests that we do look at them as pairs is contained in this guide's analysis of Canto XXXII. You have several ways to compare them.

   For instance, the two pairs offer a range of the destruction of the souls. If Dante's journey is to be a journey through the potential for evil within the soul, looking at the relationship between the sinners in each pair provides great contrast.

   Also, once you see Roger and Ugolino, your attention is pointed back at Francesca and Paolo. This might be interpreted as one of the ways that Dante creates the polar structure of his poem. Remember that this polar nature was necessary to show the way through sin to salvation—and to create the theme of the attainability of the ideal.

Test 2

1. B   2. D   3. B   4. A   5. C

6. Fairly consistently in the *Inferno*, the punishment for a sin was simply the continuation of the sin. The soul was caught in this changeless society, getting exactly what he had chosen. The symbolic retribution is this constant and eternal reminder of this choice. The discussion of the Suicides (Canto XIII) and the Thieves (Canto XXV) might give you some ideas. The images of the Flatterers (Canto XVIII) and the Sowers of Discord (Canto XXVIII) might also give you some ideas.

7. An obvious place to start would be the definition of allegory in the Symbolism and Allegory section of this guide. To set up this symbolic level of meaning, Dante does many things. Some to consider include:

   1. He uses himself as a character to show the growth in understanding.
   2. The image of Hell is the metaphoric pit. Hell is not only Hell, but the image of evil possible within the soul.
   3. Virgil is more than a literal guide.

8. Dante's literal quest would be over, but he would fail on the moral and allegorical levels. Dante would not be using reason, devout labor, or divine assistance to reach his goals. Even though he would literally be through Hell, he wouldn't have gained any understanding, enlightenment, etc. Knowing that Dante-the-author's major theme is the accessibility of Heaven through the quest, he must keep his character on the road.

9. Certainly Dante would not have approved. He might even have created specific punishments as he did for the Sodomites and the Usurers. The basis for his objection would be that these things defile the natural order of God. In Dante's view, the order and stability of his

universe depended on each person and each thing doing what he or she was intended. You might then discuss the question of whether we better maintain order and justice with or without birth control and other such "inhibitors" of natural processes, thus interpreting Dante's theme in modern terms.

10. There are several ways of approaching this question:

   1. Universality: Everyone is included and it is not possible to be excluded from the eternal spiritual life.

   2. The inclusion shows the range and grandeur and order of God's creation. By including so much, he indicates the extent and power of God.

   3. The extent of the "cast" shows the range of possible choices in the free will granted in the universe. Each individual serves as the image of a particular choice.

Term Paper Ideas

The Inferno and other works

1. Compare and contrast Dante's vision of Hell and Virgil's description of the underworld (Book VI of the *Aeneid*).

2. Compare and contrast the images of Beatrice presented in the *Vita Nuova* and in the *Comedy*.

3. How is Dante's Satan different from Milton's Satan in *Paradise Lost*?

4. What are the parallels between the story of Lancelot and Guinevere and the story of Paolo and Francesca (Canto V)?

5. In what ways is the City of Dis the antithesis of the Eternal City of the *Paradiso*?

6. Compare Dante and Aeneas in the *Aeneid*.

Dante's Philosophy

1. The *Divine Comedy* is based on a neoplatonic world view. Discuss.

2. Name and discuss several elements Dante "borrowed" from Aristotle's *Ethics*.

3. It is often said that Dante's philosophy most closely resembles that of St. Thomas Aquinas. Defend or dispute.

4. Using Virgil as an example, explain what Dante feels are the limitations of secular humanism.

Language

1. Explain Dante's use of a mixture of high and low style language.

2. Dante uses metaphor extensively, especially in the creation of his major images. Identify instances and explain their significance.

3. Ulysses' speech (Canto XXVI) seems like a set speech. Explain how and why.

Formal Elements

1. Dante uses many mythological characters in symbolic ways. Explain.

2. As one journeys deeper into Hell, the sinners are more physically bound or confined. Explain why.

3. Can the structure of Hell be seen as a visual metaphor for the deepening potential for sin? Substantiate your answer.

4. Why does Dante treat Brunetto Latini (Canto XV) differently than he treats other sinners? Does this signify any theme or nuance of Dante's philosophy?

5. What is the significance of the repeated use of the numbers 3, 9 and 10?

6. Is the *Inferno* an epic?

The Characters

1. What is the role of Beatrice?

2. Explain the literal and figurative roles of Virgil.

3. What is the relationship of Dante the pilgrim to Dante the author?

4. Is Dante the pilgrim a symbolic "everyman"?

History of the Time

1. What elements of the reigns of Pope Nicholas III and Pope Boniface VIII make Dante treat them with such venom (Canto XIX)?

2. Describe the life of the historical Beatrice.

3. Explain the details of the feud between the Ghibellines and the Guelphs.

4. What was the significance of poetry and other art forms to the Florentines of Dante's time?

Themes

1. Explain Dante's concept of sin and how it relates to free will.

2. The quest for Heaven is also a quest for order. Explain.

3. Virgil needs divine assistance at the Gates of Dis. What theme does this initiate or suggest?

Further Reading

CRITICAL WORKS

Auerbach, Eric. *Dante, Poet of the Secular World*, trans. by R. Manheim. Chicago: University of Chicago Press, 1961.

_____. "Farinata and Cavalcante" in *Mimesis*, trans. by William Trask. Princeton: Princeton University Press, 1953.

Bergin, Thomas. *Perspectives on the Divine Comedy*. New Brunswick: Rutgers University Press, 1967.

Brandeis, Irma. *The Ladder of Vision*. Garden City: Doubleday and Co., Inc., 1961.

Ciardi, John. "How to Read Dante" in *Saturday Review*, June 3, 1961.

Freccero, John, ed. *Dante: A Collection of Critical Essays*. Englewood Cliffs: Prentice-Hall, Inc., 1965.

Holmes, George. *Dante*. New York: Hill and Wang, 1980.

Quinones, Ricardo. *Dante Alighieri*. Boston: Twayne Publishers, 1979.

Glossary of Italian Characters

Many of the characters in Dante's Hell are familiar to us from the Bible or from classical mythology. One other category of Dante's sinners, however, is drawn from the Italian politics of Dante's own time. The most important of these are listed below, along with where they are placed in Hell and where they appear in the poem.

Alessio Interminei A flatterer from Lucca whom Dante recognizes in Circle VIII, bowge ii. (Canto XVIII)

Bertrand de Born Having counseled to separate a prince from his father the king, he is condemned to have his head separated from his body eternally. He is in Circle VIII, bowge ix, as a Sower of Civil Discord. (Canto XXVIII)

Bocca degli Abati In Circle IX, Antenora, is a Traitor to Country. He quarrels with Dante for trampling on his head, which is frozen into the ice, and refuses to tell the poet his name. (Canto XXXII)

Branca d'Oria A man whose soul has been consigned to Circle IX, Ptomolea, with the other Traitors to Guests, even before his body up on earth has died. (Canto XXXIII)

Brunetto Latini A Florentine scholar and author who was Dante's mentor, is placed in Circle VII with the Sodomites. (Canto XV)

Camiscion de' Pazzi A White Guelph like Dante, he has murdered a kinsman, and thus is placed in Caina, with the Traitors to Kin in Circle IX. However, since the kinsman he murdered was a traitor to his country, Camiscion claims his sin was less cruel than it seems. (Canto XXXII)

Cappochio   An alchemist placed with the Falsifiers in Circle VIII, bowge x. (Canto XXIX)

Cavalcante dei Cavalcanti   The son-in-law of Farinata degli Uberti (see below), is entombed with him eternally. Cavalcante's son, **Guido,** was a poet and a friend of Dante's. Cavalcante is a Heretic, in Circle VI. (Canto X)

Ciacco   A Florentine, whose name means "pig," he is placed in Circle III, for the Gluttonous. He offers Dante some predictions about Florentine politics, and begs to be remembered to folks at home. (Canto VI)

Farinata degli Uberti   A Florentine and an enemy of Dante's ancestors. He is the father-in-law of Cavalcante dei Cavalcanti (see above). A Heretic, Farinata is in Circle VI. (Canto X)

Filippo Argenti   A wrathful Florentine, is in Circle V, the River Styx. (Canto VIII)

Francesca da Rimini   The beautiful lady who fell in love with her brother-in-law Paolo (see below). She is whirled around with the Lustful in Circle I. (Canto V)

Friar Albergio   Frozen in the ice in Circle IX, Ptolomea. He slaughtered his brother, and is placed lower than the Traitors to Kin, among the Traitors to Guests. The Friar's body may still be alive up on earth. (Canto XXXIII)

Geri del Bello   A relative of Dante's. His violent death has not yet been avenged up on earth. He is in Circle VIII, bowge ix, with other Sowers of Discord. (Canto XXIX)

Gianni Schicchi   Impersonated a dead man in order to pass off a will that he himself would benefit from. He is placed in Circle VIII, bowge x, as an Imposter, a Falsifier. (Canto XXX)

Griffilino D'Arezzo   An alchemist placed in Circle VIII, bowge x, as a Falsifier. He mentions that the sin for which he died—basically disappointing his wealthy lord—was not as grave as the sin for which he is punished here. (Canto XXIX)

Guido da Montefeltro Ghibelline soldier who became a Franciscan monk to save his soul. He helped Pope Boniface VIII betray a political family. Although the Pope guaranteed absolution to Guido, he never truly repented and was therefore sent down to Circle VIII, bowge viii, with the Counselors of Fraud. (Canto XXVII)

Jacomo of Saint Andrea A Profligate eternally hunted in Circle VII. (Canto XIII)

Master Adam A Tuscan counterfeiter, placed with the Falsifiers in Circle VIII, bowge x. (Canto XXX)

Napoleone and Allessandro degli Alberti Two brothers who killed each other in a quarrel for their inheritance. In Circle IX, in Caina, these Traitors to Kin are frozen eternally together. (Canto XXXII)

Paolo da Rimini One of the pair of adulterous lovers (see Francesca, above) in Circle I, for the Lustful. (Canto V)

Pier da Medicina A political intriguer from Romagna. He is in Circle VIII, bowge ix, as a Sower of Civil Discord. (Canto XXVIII)

Pier della Vigne Counselor to Frederick II. He committed suicide when court gossips turned his lord against him. He is in the Wood of the Suicides, in Circle VII. (Canto XIII)

Ruggieri degli Abaldini or **Roger** The archbishop who treacherously imprisoned his ally, Count Ugolino, in a tower. He is in Circle IX, Antenora, with other Traitors to their Country. (Canto XXXIII)

Ugolino della Gherardesca A nobleman who, allied with Archbishop Ruggieri, toppled the head of a rival family from power. Ruggieri then turned on Ugolino, locking him up to starve in a tower with his sons. Some say Ugolino was finally driven to eat one of his dead sons to survive. Down in Circle IX, in Antenora, he eternally chews on Ruggieri's head in revenge. (Canto XXXIII)

Vanni Fucci   A bitter, resentful Tuscan. He is consigned to Circle VIII, bowge vii, with the Thieves, because he robbed the treasure from a sacristy. He belligerently gives Dante an obscene gesture. (Cantos XXIV–XXV)

Venedico Caccianemico   A Bolognese who sold his sister, Ghisolabella, to a rich nobleman. He has ended up in Circle VIII, bowge i, with the Panderers. (Canto XVIII)

The Critics

On Beatrice

She is an invention, but an archtypal one, appealing to the deepest emotions, which was not only to be the focus of Dante's own religious idealism but was also, in a less calculable way, to affect ideas of the relationship between art, religion, saintliness and womanhood permanently. Though made so early in his career she is in a sense Dante's most original and profound creation.

George Holmes, Dante, *1980*

The supreme work of the Middle Ages?

The *Divine Comedy* is classically referred to as the epitome, the supreme expression of the Middle Ages. If by this is meant that many typically medieval attitudes are to be found in it, it is true: the reasoning is scholastic, the learning, the mysticism are those of the author's time. But if from such a statement one is to infer (as is frequently done) that the poem is a hymn to its times, a celebration and a glorification of them, as Virgil's *Aeneid* was of Rome, then nothing could be more misleading. The *Comedy* is a glorification of the ways of God, but it is also a sharp and great-minded protest at the ways in which men have thwarted the divine plan. This plan, as Dante conceived it, was very different from the typically medieval view, which saw the earthly life as "a vale of tears," a period of trial and suffering, an unpleasant but necessary preparation for the after-life where alone man could expect to enjoy happiness. To Dante such an idea was totally repugnant. He glorified in his God-given talent, his well disciplined faculties, and it seemed inconceivable to him that he and mankind in general should not have been intended to develop to the fullest their specifically human potential. The whole *Comedy* is pervaded by his conviction that man should seek earthly immortal-

ity by his worthy actions here, as well as prepare to
merit the life everlasting.

> *Archibald T. MacAllister, Introduction
> to John Ciardi's translation of* The
> Inferno, *1954*

The inexhaustibility of Dante

The supreme art of poetry is not to *assert* meaning
but to *release* it by the juxtaposition of poetic elements. Form, in its interrelations, is the most strik-
ing element. Because in any extended poetic structure these juxtapositions when looked at from different points of vantage, that release of meaning is
subject to endless meaningful reinterpretation.
The inexhaustibility of *The Divine Comedy* is a consequence of this structural quality. It is for that reason that no one can ever finish reading it. There
will always be a new way of viewing the elements.
But if no man can finish the poem, any man can
begin it and be the richer for having begun. The
present imperfect gloss—skimming though it
be—is really about all one needs to start with. And
having started, all he needs is to pay attention. The
poem itself is the rest of the way, and the way is
marked.

> *John Ciardi, "How to Read Dante,"
> 1961*

Dante's Allegory

The greatest mistake consists in measuring Dante's allegory on the same terms as all other allego-
ries: that is, as an idea which is dressed up, a concept in figurative terms. It is precisely the contrary.
Dante moves from earth to heaven, from human
to divine. . . . He refuses to make of his figures
merely the symbols of ideas, as if they had no reality in themselves. But for him, form has a reality
precisely because it is a symbol; thus, inasmuch as
it signifies something, it is such as it is; and art is
the portrayal of this something, by which every
form lives in its allegorical essence, not as a gar-
ment but rather in its authentic reality. It is not

Grace which becomes Beatrice; it is Beatrice who lives in her essential form of divine Grace. It is clear that we have here an absolute reversal of the concept of allegory. Whoever does not understand this cannot understand Dante.

> *Luigi Pirandello*, Dante: A Collection of Critical Essays, *1965.*

Dante's Language

If we start from his predecessors, Dante's language is a well-nigh incomprehensible miracle. There were great poets among them. But, compared with theirs, his style is so immeasurably richer in directness, vigor, and subtlety, he knows and uses such an immeasurably greater stock of forms, he expresses the most varied phenomena and subjects with such an immeasurably superior assurance and firmness, that we come to the conclusion that this man used his language to discover the world anew.

> *Erich Auerbach*, Mimesis, *1953*

The Journey

If this journey to God begins in the figure of an Exodus, and then leaves that figure, to return to it after a long descent through Hell, the reason for this is clearly a matter worthy of attention. What we have here, in its simplest statement, is a first attempt to climb that fails, then a long descent that returns the wayfarer to a second attempt that succeeds. Can this configuration of event in the journey beyond be pointing to the truth that it is necessary for *us* to descend that we may ascend (this being, in the moral allegory, *our* journey)?

> *Charles Singleton*, Dante: A Collection of Critical Essays, *1965.*

Who was offended by Dante?

The Comedy, among other things, is a didactic poem of encyclopedic dimensions, in which the physico-cosmological, the ethical, the historical

political order of the universe is collectively presented; it is, further, a literary work which imitates
reality and in which all imaginable spheres of reality appear: past and present, sublime grandeur
and vile vulgarity, history and legend, tragic and
comic occurrences, man and nature; finally, it is
the story of Dante's—i.e., one single individual's—life and salvation, and thus a figure of the
story of mankind's salvation in general. Its *dramatis
personae* include figures from antique mythology,
often (but not always) in the guise of fantastic
demons; allegorical personifications and symbolic
animals stemming from late antiquity and the
Middle Ages; bearers of specific significations chosen from among the angels, the saints, and the
blessed in the hierarchy of Christianity; Apollo,
Lucifer and Christ, Fortuna and Lady Poverty,
Medusa as an emblem of the deeper circles of Hell,
and Cato of Utica as the guardian of Purgatory.
Yet, in respect to an attempt at the elevated style,
all these things are not so new and problematic as
is Dante's undisguised incursions into the realm of
real life neither selected nor preordained by aesthetic criteria. And, indeed, it is this contact with
real life which is responsible for all the verbal
forms whose directness and rigor—almost unknown in the elevated style—offended classicistic
taste.

Erich Auerbach, Mimesis, *1953*